REDEEMING RELATIONSHIPS

Healing the Brokenhearted

JOHN O'HAIR

To Jesus who has redeemed, loved, and changed me,
and to Susie who has shown me Jesus' love
and the ministry for the care for my soul.

CONTENTS

ACKNOWLEDGEMENTS

I have learned in writing this book that there are a lot of people who play parts in making a book a reality. I want to thank Adam Colwell for helping to put my thoughts to paper. Thanks to John and Patti Cepin for their ministry in our lives and passing on a model of a ministry of reconciliation and for your thoughts and improvements to the book. Thanks to Brian Murphy, Randy Reynolds, Scott and Stormy Morrison, Linda Wevodau, and Lori Bachelder for your editing and corrections. Thanks to my son's John and Ross for your encouragement to take on this task. Lastly, thanks to my soulmate and ally Susie for your love, encouragement, and modeling of these truths to me. I could not have done this without all of you.

FOREWORD

The vast majority of American Evangelicals are living in despair. Simply stated, it is because we have minimized the commission given to us by Jesus to make disciples and to teach them to do everything Jesus commanded (Matthew 28:19-20). This means, then, that we need to enter the process of transformation in Christ. The apostle Paul provides a glimpse into this process: "And we all, with unveiled face, continually seeing as in a mirror the glory of the Lord, are progressively being transformed into His image." (2 Corinthians 3:18a, AMP)

However, the emphasis to Christians has been a promise of "happiness now." As a result, when sorrow and pain come crashing into their lives, many feel betrayed—and the betrayal is real. Why? Because becoming new men and women in Christ is seldom a part of the gospel message. As a Christian marriage and family therapist for over 30 years, I have walked into enough pain, suffering, and sorrow to last several lifetimes. It often became evident that many did not understand the fullness of the gospel message, which is not only to receive salvation and become children of God, but also to put off the old man and to put on the new man in Christ, letting the Spirit of God continually renew their thoughts and attitudes through the Word of God.

This new man is to be like Christ, evidenced by a life of true righteousness and holiness (Ephesians 4:23-24). This, then, is the fullness of the Great Commission.

There are several voices crying out to change course and embrace the fullness of the Great Commission. Eugene Peterson, the late Calvin Miller, and the late Dallas Willard are among those who are calling men and women to experience a transformation in Christ *now*, not in the afterlife. In *Redeeming Relationships—Healing the Brokenhearted*, John O'Hair adds his voice to this call. Although this is his first book, his teachings are written on the hearts of his students and many others desiring to become mature in Christ. His words continue to have a transforming impact on my life and have forged within me a desire to be like Jesus.

I remember the first time I met John some 45 years ago. We were both part of a campus ministry at the University of Arizona. A group of us gathered in a dorm room to pray before venturing out to invite students to consider the claims of Christ. It was evident then—and continues to be part of John's life now—to passionately proclaim the truths of Scripture and exhort others to not only to enter His Kingdom, but be transformed into the image of God. This transformation is about redemption, reconciliation, restoration, and renewal of broken relationships.

In the pages of this book, you will discover the path to trusting God in the depths of sorrow; of holding on to hope in the midst of pain and suffering; and of having a richer understanding of forgiveness. John offers several painful parts of his story and invites us to walk with him as he came to an understanding of the impact for change they had on his life in Christ. Consider the account from John 9:1-3. Jesus' disciples asked Him, "Why was this man born blind? Was it because of his own sins or his parents' sins?" Christ answered, "It was not because of his sins or his parents' sins. This happened so the power of God could be seen in him." Every one of us has a personal narrative that invites us to embrace our stories for God's purposes to demonstrate His power and glory to the watching world.

Redeeming Relationships—Healing the Brokenhearted invites us to fully embrace our personal narratives of pain, sorrow, and guilt, to experience God's presence and unfailing love and forgiveness, and to enter into the incarnation of the Great Commission of Christ. Accept this life-changing invitation as you read.

John Cepin, M.A.
Co-founder of Journey Companions Ministries and
founder of Biblical Counseling Associates, Tucson, AZ

PROLOGUE

In 2 Corinthians 5:17-20, Paul tells us that we have been reconciled to God and that God has entrusted to us the ministry of reconciliation. This notion that we are engaged in reconciling people to God, to one another, and to ourselves is at the core of the task of a priest. Every believer is a priest. Yet the Western Church is so irrelevant in our day, in part because we do not understand reconciliation or how to foster it. I believe the irrelevance is due to our lack of understanding about our reconciliation to God and not knowing how to be reconciled to each other.

For some years now, I have asked my high school seniors, "Why did Jesus come to the planet?" Students in our Christian school tell me that Jesus came to die on the cross to save them so they can go to Heaven. When I ask if there were any other reasons He came, they tend to give me nothing more than a blank stare.

I then ask them, "If Christ came only to die for our sins, then why in John 17, during His prayer offering up His life as our redeemer-priest, does Jesus say, "I have finished the work you gave me to do?" (John 17:4) Jesus came to do more than die for us. If Heaven is the end game of His death, it tends to make all the time and activity between "praying to accept Christ" and being ushered into Heaven a waste of time.

This "plan of salvation" is limited. It tends to overemphasize getting to Heaven and doesn't do much for helping us understand the will of God to transform us into the image of His Son, and all that God is doing to conform us to that image. It also seems to discourage the idea that God is out to reconcile all of creation and bring it under the Lordship of Christ. Heaven will be here on planet Earth, not out there somewhere in the clouds. God wants to redeem and restore all the Earth to the fullness that existed prior to the Fall, and He will fully accomplish that when Christ comes back.

Dallas Willard and N.T. Wright have written about this. We evangelicals have placed such an emphasis on getting people saved and on their way to Heaven that this message has had unintended consequences; chiefly, the messiness of our current relationships and how we do not seem to care about that mess because Heaven is the objective.

Jesus came to inaugurate the Kingdom of God, to proclaim truth, to bind up broken hearts, and to restore broken relationships. I wrote this book to help us understand the ministry of reconciliation; to help us see the ways that Christ wants to redeem our relationships now. Our weak Western gospel makes it seem that we have to wait for Heaven for things to get better or to be made right. We lose sight of the reality that God is at work *now* to heal, restore, and redeem broken relationships prior to getting to Heaven. This restoration is meant to happen first in the household of the faith.

We believers are meant to trust God and look to Him to forgive, heal, and restore relationships damaged by sin.

Chapter 1 builds a foundation of who we are as image bearers of God and what that means, along with looking at some of the consequences of sin upon us and our relationships. Chapter 2 introduces the reality that God has created a cause and effect world. Our sinful choices and actions affect us and future generations. Chapter 3 looks at how our willful defiance of God and sinful choice to trust ourselves is at the core of our sin, which always leads to pain and guilt. I also reveal God's attitude toward us as we suffer from the damage of sin. Chapter 4 examines the ways we deal with the pain on our own terms, and chapter 5 surveys the ways we deal with guilt on our own terms. Chapter 6 discloses how God has taught us to trust Him with our pain and bring it to Him to comfort and heal us, while chapter 7 shares how God has taught us to bring our guilt to Him and trust Him to forgive and cleanse us. Chapter 8 offers a look at how our oaths to avoid pain or guilt are agreements Satan deceives us with to bind and destroy us. Chapter 9 closes with how our current view of the gospel inhibits good news for those who suffer.

My hope is that this book will be used by God to start or encourage you along on a pathway of trusting God with your pain and guilt—and in so doing you would taste and see that the Lord is good and embark on a ministry of reconciliation.

Chapter 1

SIN AND SORROW

As Nganga crested the hill to look through the dusty haze toward the red-orange glow where the relentless sun was mercifully retreating for the day, not even the sweet aromas of the grasses of the African savanna carried by the hot breeze from the boarding school campus below could push away the desperate longings in his heart.

Young Nganga chose with intent the direction he was facing, straining with the last of his sharp Kenyan eyesight in hopes of seeing a mere plume of smoke, anything at all, from the village of his birth. Nganga also understood that this attempt, like all of the others before it, was in vain. The village was simply too far away. In his mind's eye, he conjured up images of the mud huts with the thatched roofs in which he was raised with his twenty-one other siblings by his mother, one of the three wives of his polygamous father. He wanted to hear her voice and the cackling laughter of his brothers and sisters. He missed the familiar feel of the gritty sand on his feet, and the pungent smells from the cattle in their pens in his nostrils.

"God!" the boy cried, unable to restrain the tears. "I just want to go home."

Nganga told me that story many years later while he was living with my wife Susie and me near the Kenyatta University campus in Nairobi. We were there to teach at Rosslyn Academy, and he was in the teacher's training college at Kenyatta when he began attending a Bible study I was conducting on campus. We became fast friends, and when it came time for him to start his teaching internship, we invited him to move into our home. Nganga stayed with us for six months before departing for his first teaching job, and it was during that time that I was privileged to join him on one of his return visits to his village. In fact, I was the first white person to ever stay overnight in his village, lodging with Nganga and members of his family for three days. It was an honor and an experience I'll never forget.

> We want to make our world different than
> what it would've been had we not been there.

His story of climbing the hill and looking toward home is significant to us because it illustrates three longings, common to the human experience regardless of race or culture, that all of us feel as people who are created to be image bearers of God Himself.

> Then God said, "Let us make mankind in our image,
> in our likeness, so that they may rule over the fish in
> the sea and the birds in the sky, over the livestock and

all the wild animals, and over all the creatures that move along the ground." So God created mankind in his own image, in the image of God he created them; male and female he created them. God blessed them and said to them, "Be fruitful and increase in number; fill the earth and subdue it. Rule over the fish in the sea and the birds in the sky and over every living creature that moves on the ground." (Genesis 1:26-28)

In the Creation, God entered the darkness and chaos and brought order and light, yet I believe He left enough *undone* in the Creation because He wanted Adam and Eve, who bore His image, to step into His world and bring further order to what He had created and left undone. The Garden of Eden was not Heaven. It was not perfect. It needed to be tended. This is why God instructed the first humans to "subdue" and "rule." He wanted them to take care of what He had left undone. This is the source of the first of the three longings we have as image bearers of God: we want **to have impact**. Like our Creator, who has impact by speaking worlds and universes into existence, we are hard-wired by Him to have impact on everything and everyone around us. No one wants on their headstone, "Here lies So-and-So who did nothing." We want to make our world different than what it would've been had we not been there.

God allowed Adam and Eve to have impact on what He created by having them tend to the Garden of Eden. Even more amazing, though, is what God commissions Adam to do before Eve was created.

> Now the Lord God had formed out of the ground all the wild animals and all the birds in the sky. He brought them to the man to see what he would name them; and whatever the man called each living creature, that was its name. So the man gave names to all the livestock, the birds in the sky and all the wild animals. (Genesis 2:19-20a)

Did you catch that? God basically said to the first man, "Adam, whatever you call it, I'm going to call it. If you say 'lion,' it's a 'lion.' If it's 'chinchilla,' that's fine with me." It's not like God was out of ideas for names. Psalm 147:4-5 says God "determines the number of the stars and calls them each by name. Great is our Lord and mighty in power; his understanding has no limit." But His desire was for humans, His image bearers, to enjoy the second of the three longings: we want **to be significant.** God gave Adam's decisions about the names of the animals the same significance as if He had named them Himself. Jesus reiterated this truth about our significance when He declared to His disciples, "Truly I tell you, whatever you bind on earth will be bound in heaven, and whatever you loose on earth will be loosed in heaven." (Matthew 18:18) The Lord has chosen to allow our decisions to have incredible significance as part of who He created us to be as image bearers. I remember when my son Ross started playing in the American Youth Soccer Association. In his first game, he scored a goal. In his excitement, he ran by me on the sideline and shouted, "Dad, I tingle all over!" There's an image bearer. He did something of significance and impact, and it affected him. He got a taste of what he was made for—what he longed for.

Still, that wasn't all God that had in mind for His image bearers.

> But for Adam no suitable helper was found. So the Lord God caused the man to fall into a deep sleep; and while he was sleeping, he took one of the man's ribs and then closed up the place with flesh. Then the Lord God made a woman from the rib he had taken out of the man, and he brought her to the man. The man said, "This is now bone of my bones and flesh of my flesh; she shall be called 'woman,' for she was taken out of man." That is why a man leaves his father and mother and is united to his wife, and they become one flesh. (Genesis 2:20b-24)

It was not good for man to be alone. Humans were created to be in relationship with one another. More than that, we desire to be loved for who we are—and loved well. "What a person desires is unfailing love," Proverbs 19:22 says, with this kind of love specified in Philippians 2:3-4: "Do nothing out of selfish ambition or vain conceit. Rather, in humility value others above yourselves, not looking to your own interests but each of you to the interests of the others." This third longing of wanting **to be loved well** was placed within us by God at the very beginning and, when achieved, serves to also fulfill us as human beings. The Lord took something out of Adam to create Eve. In bringing her back to Adam, God fulfilled Adam through her. In his poetic cry of "bone of my bones and flesh of my flesh," Adam essentially looked at Eve and recognized,

"This is *me*." Likewise, a woman today often speaks of wanting to be "found" by someone. She wants to be pursued so she can ultimately be found and identified as the one who completes the other. This is why I tell young people: "Marriage is not about finding the person you can live with; it's really about finding the person you can't live without." This longing to be loved well shows itself first in our childhood relationships with our parents and other family members, but it manifests itself even further in our adolescent years. We start moving away from a need for group relationships toward a desire for a specific relationship—a best friend for life or an intimate relationship with another young man or woman—someone with whom we can share life and love together.

God's desire was for humans,
His image bearers, to want to be significant.

The evidence of this transition is attraction. As a kid in the early 1960s, I remember going to see the movie *Parent Trap* and having an immediate attraction to actress Hayley Mills. I didn't tell anyone, though. Even back then, to admit being physically attracted to another person was shied upon, as if to equate attraction to love. But they are not one and the same. Attraction, rather, is the *awakening* of what we long for, and is therefore not to be discouraged. It's something to be properly recognized and celebrated in young people. We long to be loved and are attracted by the idea of love. It's a good thing— and comes directly from how God created us.

Yet Proverbs 20:6 gives us pause. It says, "Many claim to have unfailing love, but a faithful person who can find?" Sin has come and affected us so that now, instead of being a faucet that gives and pours out to benefit a relationship, we become a drain that takes and is never filled. In our relationships, we either give to minister to someone and meet their needs, or we take to manipulate someone and meet our own narcissism. We long for love that is consistent. We want to be loved as much this morning as we were yesterday and will be tomorrow. We want to be loved unconditionally, not just when we look pretty. We want to be loved unfailingly even during those times we act ugly. So when we fail to love well, both us and the other person will feel the result of disappointment, grief, loss, and heartache; in a word, pain.

All three of these longings—to have impact, to be significant, and to be loved well—were surging through young Nganga as he looked toward his faraway village. All three originate from how we were created by God and are not something we can control. These longings cannot be turned on or turned off. Many of those who become hopeless to the point of committing suicide do so because they feel they are without impact, insignificant, and unloved. They can no longer tolerate not having these core longings fulfilled in their lives. Counselor, author, Bible teacher, and speaker Larry Crabb teaches how as image bearers we have these longings and reflect the image of God as rational, volitional, and emotional beings.

- We are rational because we reason, just like God: "Come now, and *let us reason* together," says the Lord, "Though your sins are like scarlet, they shall be as white as snow; though they are red like crimson, they shall be as wool." (Isaiah 1:18 NKJV)
- We are volitional because we choose: "*Choose for yourselves* this day whom you will serve ... as for me and my household, we will serve the Lord." (Joshua 24:15)
- We are emotional because we feel, just as God feels: "The Lord *regretted* that he had made human beings on the earth, and his heart was *deeply troubled*." (Genesis 6:6)

While we cannot change our longings, Crabb says we can affect our thinking and our choices. Sin complicates this because we have thoughts and make decisions that are either now constructive or destructive. The longings remain the same, but we try to achieve them through constructive or destructive means. We will make a difference in the lives of others—and others will, in turn, have an impact on us—depending on our thoughts and actions.

My sister Rylee is a great friend. Eighteen months younger than me, we were best buds as children, and she was a toughy; she even beat up boys who picked on me. When I was six years old, I received my first bicycle at Christmas. It was raining that day, but the next day dawned as a typical Tucson winter morning. It was clear and crisp, with a smattering of mud puddles serving as the only remnant of the previous day's storm. My sister and I went outside, and I was proud of my bike as I rode it.

She trotted up to my side. "Johnny, can I ride your bike?"

"Rylee, sure," I said as I climbed off the saddle seat. "Just don't ride it through that puddle." I pointed to a particularly large and brown body of water just off the path where I'd been riding.

What did she do? She steered directly toward and through the puddle. Brown goo clogged the treads of the fresh tires and splattered up onto the shiny frame.

To this day, I don't remember any details of Christmas morning. I don't recall how the bike was given to me, nor any of the other gifts that were under the tree. But I can vividly relive what I saw, smelled, and felt that moment the next day. Why? Because it had an impact on me. The human brain is amazing. It takes the events of our lives and files them away into conscious and unconscious memory. Certain memories are destined never to be forgotten because the event had great significance. It tells us, "I want to remember this because I treasure and want to relive that moment," or "I want to remember this because I don't want that to happen to me again." It can be positive like my son's first goal in soccer, or it can be negative like when Rylee rode my new bike through the dirty puddle. I'm certain Rylee was not intentionally trying to hurt my feelings. In her excitement to try out my bike, she probably didn't hear anything I said after, "Sure." But in giving her permission to ride my new bike with my condition of use, I longed to be respected (to have impact), listened to (to have significance), and know that I could tell my sister something and she would honor it (to be loved well). My trio of longings was violated by her action that was painful to me.

Think back right now to one of your earliest childhood memories. Have you ever asked yourself *why* you remember that particular event? What feelings come to you as you think about that event? Are they happy or sad? Identify the longing this event impacted. Many times, we are hurt not by sins of commission but sins of omission. The fact that you remember the event implies that the event matters. As victims, we need to address the damage done to us—and how that damage is affecting our thoughts and actions today. This is how victims usually become agents of similar acts. In the end, only God—the one who created us with longings that remain either unrealized or the cause of great pain—can bring the healing and fulfillment we were designed to have as His image bearers.

⌒

That fulfillment, though, is often elusive because of the dramatic events that occurred after God's glorious creation of the first man and woman. It's a familiar story that has been both inadequately understood and largely misappropriated in how men and women view each other as His image bearers.

> Now the serpent was more crafty than any of the wild animals the Lord God had made. He said to the woman, "Did God really say, 'You must not eat from any tree in the garden'?" The woman said to the serpent, "We may eat fruit from the trees in the garden,

but God did say, 'You must not eat fruit from the tree that is in the middle of the garden, and you must not touch it, or you will die.'" (Genesis 3:1-3)

Just before God created Eve from Adam, He spoke a command: "You are free to eat from any tree in the garden; but you must not eat from the tree of the knowledge of good and evil, for when you eat from it you will certainly die." (Genesis 2:16b-17) This directive was given to Adam, so what does Satan, embodied here in the serpent, go ahead and do? He went after Eve in an intentional strategy where he played, well, the devil's advocate. He asked, "Did God really say…" and she knew the answer. How? Clearly, Adam had told Eve—and a comparison of exactly what God told *him* in Genesis 2 and what *she* told Satan in Genesis 3 is revealing. Not only did she tell Satan that the tree was in the "middle" of the Garden, she said she "must not touch it." The Lord did not tell Adam either one of these tidbits of information, so we can only surmise that Adam added his own twist to God's words. "Look, Eve," he probably said as he strolled with her through the Garden. "See that tree over there, right in the middle? You must not eat it or touch it. Okay? God told me that if I eat it, we will die."

God told Adam, "Don't eat from it." Adam tells Eve, "Don't eat it or touch it." Eve communicated this to Satan, and Satan retorted then, as he always does now, with a lie—the very first lie that humans have ever heard.

"You will not certainly die," the serpent said to the woman. "For God knows that when you eat from it your eyes will be opened, and you will be like God, knowing good and evil." (Genesis 3:4-5)

If this doozy of a lie was placed on a "deception scale" of one to ten, it would score as an eleven. Satan went for the jugular. "You surely won't die. In fact, God didn't tell you the whole story. He understands that you'll see more than you do now and will actually become *like Him*. Then you'll know everything there is to know." Wow! This intrigued Eve, so much so that she made a few assumptions.

When the woman saw that the fruit of the tree was good for food and pleasing to the eye, and also desirable for gaining wisdom, she took some and ate it. She also gave some to her husband, who was with her, and he ate it. (Genesis 3:6)

There are two fascinating outcomes here. First, notice what *didn't* happen after Eve ate the fruit. She didn't die. It's possible that when Adam was first given the command not to eat from God, he expected death to be immediate. After all, God did say, "You will certainly die." Yet she didn't keel over or instantaneously turn to dust. She lived on, and not only that—she handed the fruit over to her husband and he ate, we can assume from the text, without hesitation. Yet here's where the text also says something enormously significant that is almost always overlooked: Adam *was with her*. Understand the scope of that statement. He was with Eve, likely by her side, during her entire discourse with the serpent. I believe he heard every word that was spoken and he said nothing. He didn't rise to her defense to champion or protect her. He didn't correct what she said God had said originally to him. He didn't tell the serpent to slither back to his hidey-hole or yank him over to stomp on his head. Adam failed Eve—and, by extension, failed each one of us. The Fall was not Eve's fault as is it often portrayed, and as a result, incorrectly influences how many people view men and women today. Adam was fully responsible for what happened. He could've stopped the Fall, but he didn't.

They shared the action of believing Satan's lie and disobeying God's command, and so they also shared the consequences of their action.

Then the eyes of both of them were opened, and they realized they were naked; so they sewed fig leaves together and made coverings for themselves. (Genesis 3:7)

Genesis 2 ends with a statement of blissful innocence: "Adam and his wife were both naked, and they felt no shame." (Genesis 2:25) Now innocence was lost. They *realized* they were naked and, for the very first time, they *felt* shame. The first consequence of believing the lie was that they saw their nakedness as a problem and they feel shame. It was once a gift; now it's a curse. I see this manifested all the time in teenagers. A girl will look in the mirror and say, "God doesn't love me because my eyes are too far apart. My nose is too big." God created her that way, and in truth, she's indescribably lovely to Him, yet shame tells her otherwise.

During my first high school coaching position, I was an assistant to the varsity wrestling coach. In comparison to the other teams in the city, we were a small squad in terms of weight. Our 180-pounder, Walter, was the heaviest guy we had. One day we were scheduled for a match with another school whose 180-pounder was a man-child. We were told this kid could bench press 450 pounds. He was a rock. At the behind-closed-doors weigh in, each athlete stepped onto the scale buck naked. The man-child went first, and then it was Walter's turn. As he stepped up, the other kid, the bench-press behemoth, laughed at him. We were furious. More importantly, I could tell Walter was ashamed. He shouldn't have been. He looked exactly as God created him, and he was a capable wrestler. But shame manifested itself within him because of the hurtful guffaw of his peer.

We long to be loved and are attracted
by the idea of love.

And so shame continues to affect our relationships with God and with one another, causing an estrangement that should not be. Now all the things that I long for become a problem. I can't love unfailingly. I can't be loved unfailingly. When a teenage boy chooses to go to bed with a girl, he achieves significance—but in the wrong way. He is not thinking of her best interests; he's simply making a conquest. Likewise, the girl often agrees to have sex with him because it will give her a false sense of relationship and an untrue belief that he will be her champion; she manipulates him in order to achieve this significance, but it, too, is wrong.

The second consequence of the Fall is that shame drives us to fear. Adam and Eve act out of their fear by creating the first technology (sewing) and the first fashion style (camouflage). As rational image bearers of the Creator, they reasoned that they had to cover their nakedness and saw sewing the leaves of the nearby trees together into a covering as the logical solution. They seek first to hide their nakedness—but they don't stop there.

> Then the man and his wife heard the sound of the Lord God as he was walking in the garden in the cool of the day, and they hid from the Lord God among the trees of the garden. But the Lord God called to the man, "Where are you?" He answered, "I heard you in the garden, and I was afraid because I was naked; so I hid." (Genesis 3:8-10)

Isn't it interesting? God shows up and they jump into the bushes. Their fear leads them to try to hide. It's like when my three-year-old granddaughter plays hide-and-seek with me. While I sit on my recliner and close my eyes and count to ten, she heads over to the window and positions herself behind the curtains. She thinks herself to be so clever, never realizing that when I open my eyes I can see her feet below the hem of the curtain, and watch the curtain move as she fidgets behind the cloth. She even giggles when I declare that I'm looking for her, not understanding that her expression of glee gives her position away.

Of course, I'm not angry at her for hiding that way—just as God wasn't mad at Adam and Eve for hiding the way they did, cleverly thinking that they could somehow vanish from the presence of the Almighty. God then calls out to Adam, "Where are you?" This was not for His benefit; God knew where Adam and Eve were located. The question was for Adam's benefit. He wanted him to get a realization of what was happening, and He often asks the same thing of us today when we try to tuck ourselves away from the Lord's watchful glance. Adam must've understood the context of God's question, because he didn't reply by saying, "We're over here, Lord, right behind the azaleas." No, Adam said something far more significant: "I was afraid."

Fear has now joined shame on the premises. Crabb rightly identifies fear as the core emotion for all human beings, and it originates from this moment. God then asks Adam another question that is even more significant than His first query.

And he said, "Who told you that you were naked?" (Genesis 3:11a)

One of my teams as a high school soccer coach included a midfielder who was one of three girls on the otherwise all-male squad. She went on to win a national championship at college, so her talent was unquestioned. In one game, we dominated the play so that by the end of regulation we had no less than forty-one shots on goal. The other team only had two shots on goal, but the match was still tied at zero. In overtime, we continued to be the better team thanks to the play of our star female midfielder—but it wasn't until the final minutes that we finally got the goal, scored by one of our other players, to give us the win. After the game, everyone else was celebrating, but I saw her sitting on the bench alone. She was crying.

I asked my assistant to go and ask her what was the matter, and he returned and replied, "She thinks she didn't play well."

I was incredulous. She'd played magnificently. I walked over and sat down by her side.

"Who told you that you didn't play well?" I asked gently. "Did the coaches or I say anything to lead you to believe that?" She said no. "Did any of your teammates say that at any time during the course of the game?" Again, she said no.

I repeated. "So who told you that you didn't play well?"

She never said—but it was apparent that it wasn't a person who questioned her performance on the field. You see, we have an enemy who steps into our minds, invades our consciousness, and tells us things. In the Genesis account, I'm convinced that this is the first instance of Satan speaking to the mind of a human being, but what he says hasn't changed one bit since that day long ago. He accused. "Hey Adam, guess what? You're naked. You got *nothing*. You should be ashamed of yourself. Scary, isn't it?"

You're undoubtedly familiar with the voice of the accuser. It whispers, "I'm no good at this." "I'm not pretty." "I'm a failure." True, there are times those thoughts can originate from another person or singularly from your own self-doubt. But in most cases, it is none other than Satan who is making those statements in an ongoing attempt to cause you to feel shame and fear that you shouldn't feel. Instead of thinking, "Yes, but God created me. I am His image bearer. I am precious in His sight. He is good and I rejoice in who I am," we hear and believe just the opposite.

Longings remain the same, but we try to achieve them through constructive or destructive means.

Ephesians 4:26-27 states, "'In your anger do not sin … and do not give the devil a foothold." As headmaster of Desert Christian High School, I've seen parents come in for a meeting with their child's teacher and say things that should never come out of their mouths. "You're not a very good teacher," they'll say, yet I have worked with that educator for years and seen the quality of his work day-to-day. He's an outstanding teacher, but in their anger, these parents have allowed Satan a foothold in their thinking that manifests itself in their actions. Married couples do the same thing. They'll argue and one spouse will say something to the other that's untrue and accusatory because the devil has been afforded an opportunity.

Remember when Jesus told His disciples that He must go to Jerusalem to be betrayed, suffer, and die before rising again on the third day? Peter was vehement. "'Never, Lord!' he said. 'This shall never happen to you!' Jesus turned and said to Peter, "Get behind me, Satan! You are a stumbling block to me; you do not have in mind the concerns of God, but merely human concerns.'" (Mathew 16:22b-23) Jesus wasn't saying Peter was Satan; He was acknowledging that the message out of Peter's mouth was from Satan—and He rejected it. The idea that Jesus was going to die hurt Peter. It made him angry. Pain initiated a response. But we often respond to our pain in the wrong way. When Rylee wronged me, the pain I felt caused me to say to myself, "I want respect." Even today, Satan will take that wrong response and seize upon it so that my support group introduction is, "Hello. My name is John, and I'm addicted to praise." Why? Because if I'm not careful, shame and fear can cause me to grovel at the feet of my idol of respect instead of seek my sense of respect from the high and lifted up God who created me.

Returning to the scene in Genesis, the Lord continued to question the first man—and Adam's response introduces us to a third effect of the Fall.

> "Have you eaten from the tree that I commanded you not to eat from?" The man said, "The woman you put here with me—she gave me some fruit from the tree, and I ate it." (Genesis 3:11b-12)

God does not shame us! The Lord called Adam to confess what he had done wrong, but instead Adam places blame: "The woman you put here with me..." Notice, too, that Adam blames both Eve first and then God second. "Hey, it wasn't me. It was *her*, the one *you* put with me in the first place." The Fall has made us self-protective and, therefore, no longer vulnerable in being able to love ourselves and others because it's all about finding fault. Even worse, we'll often use blame as a mechanism to turn away from our faith in God and avoid coming back to Him if we have walked away.

Genesis teaches us that we are not the originators of evil; Satan is. As His image bearers, God created us with longings that were originally being met in the Garden not in painful ways, but in fulfilling, glorious ways. The Fall doesn't take away those longings, but it has caused us to seek to meet our three core longings through destructive ways in willful defiance of the Almighty, rather than trust our good God to supply them. In Jeremiah 2, God spoke through his prophet about how Israel had forsaken Him. The Lord remembered when His people were devoted to Him as a bride is to her bridegroom, and then laments at how idolatry ate away at their love for Him until they not only turned away from Him, but rebelled against Him. Through Jeremiah, God made a declaration.

"My people have committed two sins: They have forsaken me, the spring of living water, and have dug their own cisterns, broken cisterns that cannot hold water." (Jeremiah 2:13)

Years ago, my wife and I took our boys to Tanzania, Africa to visit colleagues who were ministering the Gospel in an area near Mt. Kilimanjaro. One day they said they wanted to take us to their favorite picnic spot, and told us to bring our swimsuits. We drove out into the bush along a dirt road in the middle of the barren savanna. The great mountain provided a majestic backdrop and I was staring at the faraway peak when my wife nudged me and directed my attention to a clump of trees in the distance. In Africa, there are gallery forests that form along creeks and rivers, but this was something entirely different. We got out of the truck and walked forward until we were enveloped beneath a canopy of trees and standing at the bank of a huge pool of water. About twenty-five yards long and fifteen yards wide, it was fed by a spring that spewed from under a massive boulder. The water flowed from the spring through the pool and into a small creek. My friend told us that the pool was fifteen feet deep, yet I could see the pebbles on the bottom as vividly as if they were sitting in the palm of my hand. The water was crystal clear, and when we got into the pool, I also noticed it was delightfully warm. We swam breast-strokes against the current and had a wonderful time enjoying this pristine oasis in the middle of nowhere.

> Only God can bring the healing and
> fulfillment we were designed to have as
> His image bearers.

When I read Jeremiah 2, I think of that African spring. It's been there for thousands of years, an ever-flowing and endless supply in the wilderness, a perfect picture of what God provides for us from His eternal reservoir of love and grace—and as humans we've told Him, "I don't want that. I push you away." And if that's not bad enough, we then stubbornly walk away from the spring and stride into the desert. Before long, we realize we're thirsty, so we stop, get down on our hands and knees, and start digging at the hard, baked soil. We shove our nose into the dirt and sniff for water. We scrape a few feet deeper and smell again. We don't see water, but we can sense humidity and detect the dampness. We thrust our faces forward, press our lips into the soil, and suck at crud—determined to find what we're desperately seeking. We're out there longing to have impact, to be significant, and to be loved well, and we've chosen to fulfill them on our own and apart from God.

That's simply not possible. Crabb states that all sin is a failure to love. The Bible says, "'Love the Lord your God with all your heart and with all your soul and with all your mind.' This is the first and greatest commandment. And the second is like it: 'Love your neighbor as yourself.'" (Matthew 22:37b-39) Yet what have we done? We don't love God, and when we fail at that, we don't love one another well. When we fail to love, we sin and experience pain.

Is there hope? Romans 3:23 affirms that "all have sinned and fall short of the glory of God." Here's the great news! Jesus Christ is the only one who entered His time on planet Earth intending to have impact and significance by loving His Father well. He was determined to do all that the Father wanted Him to do, and He didn't waver. He didn't falter. He didn't sin. As a result, "all are justified freely by his grace through the redemption that came by Christ Jesus." (Romans 3:24) Through the power of God given to us by salvation in Jesus Christ, we *can* fulfill our longings and live in freedom from shame, fear, and blame and experience joy as the image bearers of God that He created us to be.

And it's possible—even in this fallen and sometimes brutal cause and effect world.

Chapter 2

CONSEQUENCES
OF CHOICE

Physicist and mathematician Sir Isaac Newton was one of the most influential scientists of all time. Born in England on Christmas Day 1643, Newton approached his work with a worldview that the God who created the universe was good, reasonable, and rational. This God, Newton assumed, organized the universe in such a way that it could be studied and understood. He was not like the early Greeks who believed that if they investigated the universe too far they'd open up a Pandora's Box of evil. Rather, Newton believed discoveries could be made about the universe without upsetting the fabric of the cosmos in the process.

In His *Philosophiae Naturalis Principia Mathematica* (Mathematical Principles of Natural Philosophy), Newton presented essential concepts of physics including a description of bodies in motion in three basic laws: 1) a stationary body will stay stationary unless an external force is applied to it; 2) force is equal to mass times acceleration, and a change in motion is proportional to the force applied; and 3) for every action, there is an equal and opposite reaction. These principles of *cause and effect* are undeniable realities.

It's interesting, then, that one of Newton's most famous quotes is this: "I can calculate the motion of heavenly bodies, but not the madness of people." As human beings, we try to wish away or delude ourselves to the reality of cause and effect. How? Every decision we make has a consequence. Every time we sin, there will be a consequence, and oftentimes that consequence is unintended or far more harmful than we could ever imagine. So what do we tend to do? When we do something wrong, or even have something wrong done to us, we strive to deny the consequences. We want to negate the reality of cause and effect.

I recall one time I desperately wanted to remove the consequences of my sin. It was when I was asked to be the public address announcer at one of our school's baseball games. The principal also served as the school's varsity baseball coach, and among his starting nine players was a kid who was quite skinny, no different than I was back in my high school days. As his turn came to bat and he walked up to home plate, I decided to add some levity to my player introduction. I opened the microphone, said his uniform number and name, then quipped, "And, as you can see, he's not on steroids."

As he was about to step into the batter's box, the young man turned and looked right at me at the announcer's table. The hurt I saw on his face was devastating. I knew I'd blown it, big time. I would've done anything to take my words back, and

I certainly wished I could've taken away the wound I caused to the student's self-esteem. Even worse, the incident happened in front of a grandstand full of people, and because a game had to be played, I couldn't go up to the young man and apologize right away. I had to wait until the game was over.

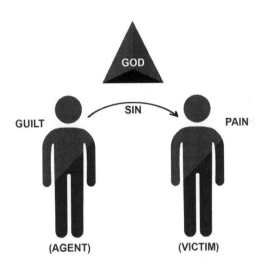

Two things happened in the incident that occurs every time one human being (the agent) sins against another human being (the victim).

- As the *agent*, I felt *guilt* for my sin. The level of guilt felt varies in type and amount according to the level of the sin committed. It is proportional. In my case, the guilt I felt was heightened by the fact that it was done to a young person and in a public setting. I originally didn't intend my attempt at humor to cause any offense, but intentions often don't matter once the sin is committed.

- As the *victim*, the young man felt *pain* because he was sinned against. The level of pain, too, varies in type and amount according to the level of the act committed. It is also proportional. In his case, the pain he felt was heightened by the fact that it was said by a trusted adult and in front of a large group of people and peers.

For both of us, the agent who felt guilt and the victim who felt pain, cause and effect were immediate and undeniable. This is not only a universally human experience confirmed by the very laws of the universe; it is an experience that is constantly overseen by the Creator of that universe. We sin against people, we are being sinned against by people—and God is aware of all of it. But He's not just a spectator watching these human interactions with an uninvolved eye, as deists believe. On the contrary, God uses each one of these experiences to work it together for good for those who love Him (Romans 8:28).

꒜

Let's look at two accounts from the Bible that shows how God, in His sovereignty, works in the lives of agents and victims— the first occurring after the departure of Adam and Eve from the Garden of Eden. The players in this real-life drama are their sons Cain and Abel.

"Now Abel kept flocks, and Cain worked the soil. In the course of time Cain brought some of the fruits of the soil as an offering to the Lord. And Abel also brought an offering—fat portions from some of the firstborn of his flock. The Lord looked with favor on Abel and his offering, but on Cain and his offering he did not look with favor. So Cain was very angry, and his face was downcast. Then the Lord said to Cain, 'Why are you angry? Why is your face downcast? If you do what is right, will you not be accepted? But if you do not do what is right, sin is crouching at your door; it desires to have you, but you must rule over it.'" (Genesis 4:2b-7)

For both of us, the agent who felt guilt and the victim who felt pain, cause and effect were immediate and undeniable.

An act of sin is always precipitated by a misappropriated emotion. Here Cain becomes angry because his offering was not accepted by God, but Abel's was accepted. Why? In Hebrews 11:4, we learn that it was by *faith* that Abel brought a better offering than Cain did—and by faith Abel was commended as righteous, because "without faith it is impossible to please God." (Hebrews 11:6a) Faith is the key. Abel's offering was made with an attitude of faith and therefore elicited God's favor, so we can infer that Cain's offering was *not* made by faith but instead with some different motivation. Since Cain was a farmer, I believe his offering was intended as a bribe to God. "I'll give you my offering," Cain said, "and in return you'll give me rain and a good harvest." Cain was not giving to

43

please God; he was giving to please himself and to get what he wanted. When he didn't get God's favor—when he found out God wasn't going to accept his bribe—he got mad.

The book of James says this: "What causes fights and quarrels among you? Don't they come from your desires that battle within you? You desire but do not have, so you kill. You covet but you cannot get what you want, so you quarrel and fight. You do not have because you do not ask God. When you ask, you do not receive, because you ask with wrong motives." (James 4:1-3a) As human beings, we want something, and if we don't get it, we react. Using this passage of scripture as the foundation, Crabb talks about the difference between goals and desires. A **goal**, he says, is something we want that we *can* control. For example, Ephesians 5:25 tells husbands to love their wives. Men can control that by doing it. A **desire**, on the other hand, is identified by Crabb as something we want that we *cannot* control. Husbands want their wives to love them in return. Men can't control that, however. There's only one thing we can do, then, with something we desire, and that is we can take it to God in prayer, lay it at His feet, and submit to His answer of "yes," "no," or "not yet." We choose to abide by His will for that desire. We trust and rely on God. We have faith.

Crabb rightly states, then, that we don't like to keep things as desires because that requires us to trust God, not ourselves, for the outcome—so we tend to *shift* what we want from a desire to a goal. We are not going to have faith in God, so we're going to take over to get what we want. This shift causes the husband to say, "I'm going to make my wife love me." If you say that statement out loud, it sounds crass and ugly—because it is. It's manipulation. How does this play out? Let's say the husband brings home flowers, makes dinner, and cleans up the kitchen as acts of love toward his wife, but then later, when he asks his wife if they can make love, she says she is tired and has a headache. If wanting his wife to love him is a desire submitted to God in faith, he'll feel sorrow and sadness at her response. It'll cause him pain, but he is motivated to love her well. However, if he has shifted wanting his wife to love him to a goal, he'll feel anger and resentment at her response. He fails to love her. This kind of anger is an idiot light that says to our hearts, "Something is wrong here. You are not trusting God."

Cain's response of anger was evidence that he was not willing to submit to God's response to his bribe-directed offering. So what did Cain do as a result of his anger? He chose not to love his brother.

> "Now Cain said to his brother Abel, 'Let's go out to the field.' While they were in the field, Cain attacked his brother Abel and killed him." (Genesis 4:8)

The Bible is poignant in its simplicity. We don't receive a graphic account of the incident or details that could aid a crime scene investigation of the event. The first murder in the history of planet Earth was stated rather matter-of-factly. Cain the agent has committed the sin, and Abel the victim has been sinned against to the point of death. So God, who was overseeing the entire scene, asks some questions.

> "Then the Lord said to Cain, 'Where is your brother Abel?' 'I don't know,' he replied. 'Am I my brother's keeper?' The Lord said, 'What have you done? Listen! Your brother's blood cries out to me from the ground.'" (Genesis 4:9-10)

Just like he did with Adam, God asks these questions not to seek information but to make Cain aware of what was really going on. Cain's response to the first question from the Lord is dripping with contempt. He is trying to hide away from his sinful action and push God away from him. The second question was asked so that Cain might admit to what he did and seek forgiveness for his moral failure—but we see no response from Cain to that query. He apparently did not confess or repent. So cause and effect takes place. God brings a consequence to Cain's lack of faith.

> "When you work the ground, it will no longer yield its crops for you. You will be a restless wanderer on the earth." (Genesis 4:12)

God smacks away Cain's crutch: his skills as a farmer. Yet this consequence from God was not punitive. It was intended to be redemptive. How? It provided Cain another opportunity to trust and rely on God. The Lord even replies to Cain's ironic fear that he could be murdered by declaring that no one will be allowed to kill him. So what did Cain do? He "went out from the Lord's presence and lived in the land of Nod, east of Eden. Cain made love to his wife, and she became pregnant and gave birth to Enoch. Cain was then building a city, and he named it after his son Enoch." (Genesis 4:16-17) Instead of remaining a wanderer that could lead to his redemption, Cain rooted himself to the ground again—not as a farmer, but as a builder. Cain attempted to "work around" God's punishment and said once more, "I will not trust God. I will not submit!" Even in the loving discipline and mercy of the Lord, Cain ultimately refuses to bow his knee.

> An act of sin is always precipitated
> by a misappropriated emotion.

The second account from the Bible I'd like to focus upon that shows how God, in His sovereignty, works in the lives of agents and victims is one of the lesser told tales from the book of Genesis. It involves Abraham and his wife Sarah, and Abimelek the king of Gerar. In ancient times, it was common for kings to take as a possession unmarried women who came into their kingdom's boundaries and add them to his harem. This was done by kings to build political ties of favor with individuals or nations. When approached by Abimelek, Abraham told him that Sarah was his sister, not his wife, and so she was taken away. Why did Abraham do this? Back when he was about to enter into Egypt as God had instructed him to do, he said to Sarah, "I know what a beautiful woman you are. When the Egyptians see you, they will say, 'This is his wife.' Then they will kill me but will let you live. Say you are my sister, so that I will be treated well for your sake and my life will be spared because of you." (Genesis 12:11b-13) Abraham simply wanted to save his skin. He turned his desire to be safe in Egypt, something he couldn't control, into a goal that he could try to control—and in doing so, he failed to trust God. As a result, Sarah is wrongly in the possession of Abimelek. But God still knows what is going on, so He again intervenes.

> "God came to Abimelek in a dream one night and said to him, 'You are as good as dead because of the woman you have taken; she is a married woman.'" (Genesis 20:3)

Abraham is the agent who commits the sin of deception, and Abimelek is the victim who has been sinned against unknowingly—until the Lord reveals it to him. Upon hearing the news, Abimelek understandably launches his defense.

> "Now Abimelek had not gone near her, so he said, 'Lord, will you destroy an innocent nation? Did he not say to me, "She is my sister," and didn't she also say, "He is my brother"? I have done this with a clear conscience and clean hands.' Then God said to him in the dream, 'Yes, I know you did this with a clear conscience, and so I have kept you from sinning against me. That is why I did not let you touch her. Now return the man's wife, for he is a prophet, and he will pray for you and you will live. But if you do not return her, you may be sure that you and all who belong to you will die.'" (Genesis 20:4-7)

Incredibly, the sovereign God knew what was going on all along and allowed events to progress so that He could test the faith not of Abraham, but of Abimelek. God "did not let" Abimelek touch Sarah, preventing Abimelek from sinning against Him. Now, God gives Abimelek a choice that will reveal if the king truly trusts Him or not. Return Sarah, and you will live; do not return Sarah, and you and everyone around you will die. In His dealings with Cain, God tried to draw the agent of sin to a place of faith in Him. Here, God is doing the exact same thing through the life circumstances of the *victim* of sin. This is how God operates—dictating or allowing situations to take place in our lives with the express goal of giving us the chance, and the choice, to trust in Him. We tend to think that when someone sins against us or against someone else that we love, God is not in control. "If God was a loving God," the enemy will whisper, "He wouldn't have allowed that to happen." It's an understandable thought, but it is not a biblical one. It's based on an incorrect presupposition that God doesn't allow hurt on those He loves; yet pain and sorrow are an essential part of the Christian experience, and they serve to reveal the love and trustworthiness of God as much as joy and happiness do. The truth is it doesn't matter if we have committed the sin or are the recipient of another's sinful act—God will always use it to give us an opportunity to believe in and rely upon Him.

So what did Abimelek choose? After what was likely a sleepless night, Abimelek responded quickly and decisively.

"Early the next morning Abimelek summoned all his officials, and when he told them all that had happened, they were very much afraid. Then Abimelek called Abraham in and said, 'What have you done to us? How have I wronged you that you have brought such great guilt upon me and my kingdom? You have done things to me that should never be done.' And Abimelek asked Abraham, 'What was your reason for doing this?' Abraham replied, 'I said to myself, "There is surely no fear of God in this place, and they will kill me because of my wife." Besides, she really is my sister, the daughter of my father though not of my mother; and she became my wife. And when God had me wander from my father's household, I said to her, "This is how you can show your love to me: Everywhere we go, say of me, "He is my brother.""' (Genesis 20:8-13)

Abimelek wasted no time. He gathered all of his court early in the morning, told them about the dream without hesitation (indicating that he believed the experience was legitimate, not just a random musing of his subconscious mind), and they, too, reacted with concern and fear. This showed that his officials also revered the Lord. Abimelek the victim then called Abraham the agent to task. He used piercing questions that, just as God did with Adam and Cain, were intended to bring Abraham to an awareness of what he and his sinful choice had wrought. "What have you done?" "How have I wronged you?" "Why did you do this?" Notice, too, how Abimelek's concern was not for himself alone; he knew that *all* of the people under his rule were affected as well. That's what sin does—it has an unmistakable trickle down impact on the lives of many. Abimelek wanted Abraham to understand that his actions placed a king and his entire kingdom on the path to eradication.

Finally, Abimelek's discourse to Abraham included one non-query statement that is significant: "You have done things to me that should never be done." When we confront others with the sin they have committed against us, we're often told to forgive them and then move on—but that's not what Scripture directs us to do. Luke 17:3 states, "If your brother or sister sins against you, rebuke them; and if they repent, forgive them." This shows that our expression of forgiveness to our offender is supposed to be *conditional*. We are to forgive *if* they repent. We should not forgive them prior to repentance on their part. Why? Because they need to understand that they have done things to us that should never have been done. Only when they come to that realization can they therefore be positioned to fully appreciate and accept our act of forgiveness towards them.

God, in His sovereignty,
works in the lives of agents and victims.

Abimelek wanted Abraham to see that his sin of deception had consequences far beyond an attempt to preserve his own life. Yet Abraham responds not with repentance, but with excuses. The first shows his incorrect presupposition ("I said to myself, 'There is surely no fear of God in this place...'"), and the second tries to justify his lie ("Besides, she really is my sister, the daughter of my father though not of my mother…").

Abraham has done a horrible thing to his wife by making her part of his self-preservation tactic and devaluing and endangering her life, and he has done a horrible thing to Abimelek and his kingdom by placing them under a death sentence. But he doesn't recognize either one here. Instead, he tries to reason away his sin.

Since Abraham doesn't repent, Abimelek doesn't forgive him, either—but he does do what God told him to do. He returned Sarah to Abraham, and then some.

"Then Abimelek brought sheep and cattle and male and female slaves and gave them to Abraham, and he returned Sarah his wife to him. And Abimelek said, "My land is before you; live wherever you like." To Sarah he said, "I am giving your brother a thousand shekels of silver. This is to cover the offense against you before all who are with you; you are completely vindicated." Then Abraham prayed to God, and God healed Abimelek, his wife and his female slaves so they could have children again, for the Lord had kept all the women in Abimelek's household from conceiving because of Abraham's wife Sarah." (Genesis 20:14-18)

Though Abraham sinned against Abimelek (a sin of commission, in that it was intentional), Abimelek recognized that he sinned against both Abraham and God (a sin of omission, in that it wasn't intentional). Yet more than recognize this reality, Abimelek took full responsibility for it with a generous act of restitution that showed his *genuinely repentant* heart. In Matthew 3:8, John the Baptist exhorted the Pharisees and Sadducees to "produce fruit in keeping with repentance." That's precisely what Abimelek did here—and he modeled a tremendous truth for those of us who assume that we only have to deal with intentional sin done by us or to us. We cannot ignore sin that is unintentional. Whether we are the agents or victims of sins of omission, God desires for us to recognize the sin and respond to it appropriately.

The story from Genesis 20 ends with the sovereign God keeping the promise made in Abimelek's dream. Abraham prayed for Abimelek, and the king and all of his people lived as an additional consequence of Abraham's sin being removed: Abimelek's wife and female slaves had been prevented from having children. It is another sobering reminder that sin will have repercussions far beyond what we think when we reason to ourselves, "Oh, this little sin won't hurt anybody."

When Moses took the stone tablets up Mt. Sinai for the Lord in Exodus 34, God passed in front of Moses and declared who He is as He revealed this: "The Lord, the Lord, the compassionate and gracious God, slow to anger, abounding in love and faithfulness, maintaining love to thousands, and forgiving wickedness, rebellion and sin. Yet he does not leave the guilty unpunished; he punishes the children and their children for the sin of the parents to the third and fourth generation." The truth expressed by the Lord in the last sentence of His proclamation was literally lived out through Abraham, Isaac, and Jacob, three men and their families who shared the same dysfunctional sin: they were liars.

That shouldn't surprise us, though. All of us have family sin of one kind or another, and it is in the redemptive nature of God to break the cycle of that sin—but it requires someone to step up and be genuinely repentant. How this played out in the lives of the patriarchs of our faith is compelling. It starts with an almost play-by-play repeat of Abraham's sin by his son Isaac involving his wife Rebekah. Told in Genesis 26, Isaac goes to Gerar and meets another Abimelek. Isaac must've heard the tale of his father's lie, because when the men there asked him about his wife, he told them she was his sister. He, too, feared for his life. She was presumably taken into Abimelek's court, but the king knew something was awry when he looked down from a window one day and saw Isaac caressing her in an intimate fashion. Abimelek confronted Isaac. "She really is your wife! ... What is this you have done to us?" This Abimelek, perhaps remembering the story of Abraham and Sarah from his predecessor, then gave orders to all the people: "Anyone who harms this man or wife shall surely be put to death."

All of us have family sin of one kind or another, and it is in the redemptive nature of God to break the cycle of that sin.

Issac went on to father Jacob and Esau, and his predisposition toward deception carried forward to them. Jacob was a homebody and learned to skillfully cook; Esau was a hunter and preferred the open country. When Esau returned home from a particularly long hunt exhausted and near starvation, he asked for the bread and lentil stew Jacob had prepared. Jacob seized the opportunity, denying his brother food unless he first agreed to sell him the birthright Esau had acquired by being the firstborn son. Famished, Esau agreed—instantly willing to give up his birthright to satisfy his appetite—and immediately regretted his decision and despised his brother. As the boys continued to grow into young men, their parents played favorites. Rebekah preferred Jacob while Isaac was partial to Esau. When Isaac was old and could hardly see, he decided to make sure Esau, robbed earlier of his birthright, was going to get the blessing he should've had all along. In that culture, the blessing ceremony was supposed to include the entire clan, but Isaac decided he was going to keep the blessing secret, perpetrating more deception. He told Esau to go, hunt wild game, and return and prepare it the way he liked. Once he ate, he promised to give Esau the blessing. Esau chose to participate in the deception of the clan and left for the country.

It just so happened that Rebekah overheard everything. She knew after all of these years of marriage that she couldn't trust the old badger, so she came up with a lie of her own. She instructed Jacob to go to the flock and bring her two choice goats so she could cook up the savory meal Isaac craved—and then have Jacob deliver it to him before Esau returned so that he, and not Esau, received the blessing. Jacob, too, was fine with the lie, but he saw holes in her plan. "But my brother Esau is a hairy man while I have smooth skin. What if my father touches me? I would appear to be tricking him and would bring down a curse on myself rather than a blessing." (Genesis 27:12) In response, Rebekah took Esau's best clothes and put them on Jacob. She also covered his hands and the smooth part of his neck with goatskins to duplicate Esau's hairy physique. The deception became more elaborate. Then Jacob went in to Issac.

"My father."

"Yes, my son," Isaac answered. "Who is it?"

"I am Esau your firstborn. I have done as you told me. Please sit up and eat some of my game, so that you may give me your blessing."

Isaac, being a good liar, smelled a rat. "How did you find it so quickly, my son?"

Jacob appealed to his father's faith to season his lying response. "The Lord your God gave me success," he replied.

"Come near," Isaac insisted, "so I can touch you to know whether or not you really are my son Esau." Jacob did as he was told. "The voice is the voice of Jacob," Isaac reasoned, "but the hands are the hands of Esau." He asked Jacob again, "Are you really my son Esau?"

"I am," Jacob lied.

Jacob brought the food to Isaac, he ate and drank some wine, and then, just to make sure, Isaac said, "Come here, my son, and kiss me." Jacob did, and when Isaac caught the smell of his clothes, he was convinced—and delivered the blessing. Jacob left, no doubt with a happy Rebekah watching from behind the tent flap, and moments later Esau arrived.

"Who are you?" Isaac asked. "I am your son," he answered, "your firstborn, Esau." Suddenly, Isaac *trembled violently*. His attempt to deceive the clan and get what he wanted had back-fired. He was caught in his own sin. "Who was it, then, that hunted game and brought it to me? I ate it just before you came and I blessed him—and indeed he will be blessed!"

And so it went—from Abraham to Isaac to Jacob and through their families: lying was commonplace. Eventually, Jacob's name was changed by God to Israel after he had an encounter with God that led him to have faith in the God of his fathers. But even then, Israel didn't respond with an act of genuine repentance for the family's generational sin of decep-tion. What happened next, then, should've been expected. Israel's sons despised their brash and favored younger brother Joseph because he bragged about having crazy dreams of rul-ing over them, so they devised a deception that was to result in Joseph's murder. It is well worth your time to read the entire biblical account of Joseph's life in Genesis chapters 37-50, even if a critical moment is missing from the text. For it is after the brothers, instead of leaving Joseph at the bottom of a cistern to die, decided to sell him to a Midianite merchant caravan headed to Egypt, that Joseph had his own encounter with God that *brought* repentance and *broke* the cycle of sin in his family. I believe this pivotal event occurred sometime during the cara-van trip to Egypt. The Bible doesn't share the scene with us, but it had to have happened then—because it was afterward, when Joseph the slave was faced with his chance to lie and sin with the lusty wife of his master Potiphar, that he said these words.

"With me in charge," he told her, "my master does not concern himself with anything in the house; everything

he owns he has entrusted to my care. No one is greater
in this house than I am. My master has withheld nothing from me except you, because you are his wife. How
then could I do such a wicked thing and sin against
God?" (Genesis 39:8b-9)

Joseph did not want to lie. More significant, he did not want
to sin against God. A lot of good it did him: Joseph was thrown
into jail by her false accusations against him, and he remained
in prison even after his ability to interpret dreams presented
opportunities for his release that were either ignored or forgotten. Yet through it all Joseph maintained his integrity before
others and the Lord. He did not lie. He pleased God. Ultimately,
he is brought to a place of authority in Egypt, second-in-com-
mand to the Pharaoh himself. In a time of famine, Joseph's
planning and leadership made it so that "all the world came to
Egypt to buy grain from Joseph, because the famine was severe
everywhere." (Genesis 41:57) Among those who came were
Joseph's brothers—and his tender and dramatic interaction
with the same siblings who once wanted to kill him resulted in
these words, one of the greatest quotes in all of the Bible.

"You intended to harm me, but God intended it for
good." (Genesis 50:20a)

Joseph, the victim of sin time and again, realized that his
Almighty God was indeed fully aware, fully involved, and fully
sovereign throughout every single event of his life, even those
that brought suffering and were painful and unfair. Therefore,

Joseph became an agent not of sin but of *healing and hope* to his family. Because of his genuine repentance of his family's generational sin of deception, and because of his continual utter trust and reliance on God, Joseph became a man whose behavior, most Bible scholars agree, was a precursor of what Jesus Christ accomplished centuries later.

> Every Christian can live in freedom from shame,
> fear, and blame as His image bearers.

I believe every family has a person in it that can break the cycle of family sin. I believe every Christian can decide to give their longings to have impact, to have significance, and to be loved well and turn them over to a God they can trust. Every Christian can live in freedom from shame, fear, and blame as His image bearers. Every Christian can do this in a brutal cause and effect world by dedicating the goals they can control and the desires they can't control to a God who dictates or allows every situation as an opportunity to rely upon Him.

And it's all a matter of trust.

Chapter 3

SHAPING
OUR IMAGE

American journalist and humorist Helen Rowland once said that "falling in love consists merely in uncorking the imagination and bottling the common sense." Perhaps, but time and again I've listened as Christian students, their bright eyes gleaming, tell me that they are in love. Usually, my first question is, "Is he (or she) a believer in Jesus?" After a brief hesitation, they'll often respond, "No—not yet." I'll then explain how God says in the Bible that it's not wise to be in that kind of a relationship with an unbeliever. Surprised at my seeming lack of enthusiasm for their experience with love's first bloom, they just nod or look at me with an expression that screams, "Yeah, Mr. O'Hair—but I know what I'm doing. I know what's best for me."

I've seen that same expression on the faces of adult men who come into my office, briefly review the problems with their marriage, and then announce, "John, I'm going to get a divorce. I just don't love my wife anymore, and God wants me to be happy." Those wedding day vows to love and cherish "for better, for worse, for richer, for poorer, in sickness and in health, until death do us part" are suddenly trumped by a self-centered mindset that says, "My happiness is more important. Besides, I know what's better for me far more than God does."

It is a dangerous thing to trust in yourself instead of in the Lord.

Proverbs 28:26 is a telling verse of Scripture that actually defines what makes a person a fool. It says, "Those who trust in themselves are fools, but those who walk in wisdom are kept safe." Juxtapose that with this passage from earlier in the same book: "Trust in the Lord with all your heart and lean not on your own understanding; in all your ways submit to him, and he will make your paths straight." (Proverbs 3:5-7) The difference between being wise and being foolish is found in *who you trust*. I often have my students look up synonyms for the word "trust." It's a great exercise. They'll find responses such as, "to rely upon," "to depend upon," "to have confidence in," "to believe," and "to have faith." *Trust* is a word that still has an edge to it that has somehow been lost in the words belief and faith, which in today's culture have taken on a more nebulous, existential meaning—that our choice ""to believe or "have faith" is not based on anything concrete nor will produce any substantive action. As author and social critic Os Guinness says in his book *Fit Bodies, Fat Minds*, his treatise on the dumbing down of evangelicalism through popular culture, we can believe something, but it no longer demands any certain way of reacting.

Still, Jesus taught in Matthew 6:24, "No one can serve two masters. Either you will hate the one and love the other, or you will be devoted to the one and despise the other." Christ concluded the thought with the words, "You cannot serve both God and money," but the one-or-the-other principle of the two masters applies across the board. Jesus is the one who made it binary. If you love this master, you will hate the other. If you are devoted to one, you will despise the other. Therefore, to trust in yourself is folly; to trust in the Lord is wisdom. There is no in-between.

> Choosing whom you will trust occurs
> moment by moment each and every day.

Choosing whom you will trust occurs moment by moment each and every day. Why? Because folly is ingrained in every one of us as human beings. Proverbs 27:22 provides this graphic insight: "Though you grind a fool in a mortar, grinding them like grain with a pestle, you will not remove their folly from them." It paints a rather hopeless picture, doesn't it? Yet what is impossible with us is possible with God. He removes our folly every time we choose to trust in Him. After all, central to the redemptive work of Jesus Christ on the cross is that He came, died, and rose again to save us from ourselves. The Lord is relentless in His task of getting us away from trusting ourselves.

A familiar story from the Bible illustrates this—but only after you see it in a way you've likely never seen it before. Jesus was approached by a "certain ruler" whose identity we know nothing more about, except that he was wealthy. He asked, "Good teacher, what must I do to inherit eternal life?" The Lord answered:

> "'Why do you call me good?' Jesus answered. 'No one is good—except God alone. You know the commandments: 'You shall not commit adultery, you shall not murder, you shall not steal, you shall not give false testimony, honor your father and mother.'" (Luke 18:19-20)

Take notice of the man's query, "What must I do..." The rich ruler came into the conversation brimming with self-confidence, and why not? He was a self-made man who had placed his trust in himself and his abilities. Knowing this, Jesus' response first placed the focus where it needed to be. *No one* is good—except God. He then listed some of the commandments He discerned this ruler knew, all to illicit the reply from him that allowed Jesus to challenge the ruler to the very core of his being.

> "'All these I have kept since I was a boy,' he said.
> When Jesus heard this, he said to him, 'You still lack one thing. Sell everything you have and give to the poor, and you will have treasure in heaven. Then come, follow me.'
> When he heard this, he became very sad, because he was very wealthy. Jesus looked at him and said,

'How hard it is for the rich to enter the kingdom of God! Indeed, it is easier for a camel to go through the eye of a needle than for someone who is rich to enter the kingdom of God.'" (Luke 18:21-25)

Do you see it? The man trusted *in his ability* to earn eternal life—in much the same way some wealthy people today feel that all they have to do is purchase the best attorney or buy off the right influence to get what they want. This is folly. That's why Jesus told him, "Sell everything you have..." He had to give up everything he trusted in—his wealth and his ability to acquire and keep that wealth—and trust solely in God. The man couldn't do it, and that prompted Jesus to affirm to him and all who were listening just how difficult it is for a person who trusts in themselves and what they possess to inherit eternal life; it's impossible. Well, almost:

"Those who heard this asked, 'Who then can be saved?' Jesus replied, "What is impossible with man is possible with God.'" (Luke 18:26-27)

God wants us to trust Him alone. That's what He's after; that's what brings us and Him joy! Yet in the book *TrueFaced*, co-author John Lynch says that we often trust in ourselves to try to make God happy when in reality we should simply be trusting in God—and that the choice of reliance in Him by itself will please Him. Hebrews 11:6 states it so well: "Without faith it is impossible to please God."

Trusting in ourselves can be hurtful and is always

ineffective. When he was dying of lymphoma cancer, Christian philosopher Francis Schaeffer once told of someone saying to him, "If you only have faith, you will be healed." How cruel—as though if it were up to Francis, he wouldn't have cancer. That's ludicrous, and it diminishes what God in His sovereignty was accomplishing through Schaeffer's life as he endured the cancer. Likewise, many Christians think that if they pray in just the right way, using the correct "magic words," that they will get what they ask for. That's simply not true. Martin Luther said, "Prayer is not overcoming God's reluctance. It is laying hold of His willingness." Healing and answers to prayer come not by trusting in yourself, but in choosing to trust in God— relying upon, depending upon, having confidence in, and believing and having faith in Him alone. It's in saying, "God, you know what is best for me."

~~

The Apostle Paul understood that God knew what was best for him, but his perspective is most telling because of his circumstances. Many Christians mistakenly believe Paul went around with a smile on his face and a skip in his step, rejoicing in the Lord and acting like some kind of biblical superhero, nary a care in the world. But that is far from the reality. In this passage from his letter to the believers in Corinth, Paul refers to some of the difficulties he suffered, and he didn't mince any words.

"We do not want you to be uninformed, brothers and sisters, about the troubles we experienced in the province of Asia. We were under great pressure, far beyond our ability to endure, so that we despaired of life itself. Indeed, we felt we had received the sentence of death". (2 Corinthians 1:8-9a)

Whatever happened there was so bad that Paul would've rather died than to face it. We know that among the hardships he endured after becoming a Christian were no less than three floggings. This was a horrific punishment. Performed with a short whip made of two or three leather thongs knotted with small chunks of metal, bone, or heavily indented pieces of bronze, flogging or scourging quickly removed the skin from the body. Sometimes the Roman scourge contained a hook at the end that was fittingly called a "scorpion." The victim was usually made to stoop, resulting in deeper lashes from the shoulders to the waist. Lacerations, torn flesh, exposed muscles, and excessive bleeding brought the victim to the point of death. This is solely conjecture, but I believe Paul was speaking in 2 Corinthians 1 of his second or third flogging. I can't imagine the pain of the moment, much less the long recovery process. It must've been excruciating.

> Trusting in ourselves can be hurtful
> and is always ineffective.

Confronted with even the idea of experiencing that kind of suffering, most of us would be unwilling to face it, much less try to find purpose in it. But not Paul. Look at these incredible words. Read them slowly and allow them to enter your heart.

"But this happened that we might not rely on ourselves but on God, who raises the dead." (2 Corinthians 1:9b)

This verse changed my entire philosophy on suffering. God permitted Paul to go through this so that Paul could learn not to trust in himself. How committed is our Lord to breaking us from trusting ourselves? To the point of allowing us to go through exceedingly painful moments so that we will learn to ask, "Am I going to trust me, or am I going to trust God?"

In his book *The Problem of Pain*, C.S. Lewis says that "pain insists upon being attended to. God whispers to us in our pleasures, speaks in our consciences, but shouts in our pains. It is his megaphone to rouse a deaf world." Lewis also teaches that pain convinces us that we are not in control, yet the fool in us wants to take over in the midst of our pain to make a way to get out of it. We're so committed to escape because we've come to believe something about pain that simply isn't true. We think pain is death—yet Paul concludes that God has all the power He needs during our suffering to deal with our pain.

Why does Paul have this remarkable perspective? He understands the character and attributes of God. Here's what he told the Corinthians *before* he shared about his sufferings.

"Praise be to the God and Father of our Lord Jesus Christ, the Father of compassion and the God of all comfort, who comforts us in all our troubles, so that we can comfort those in any trouble with the comfort we ourselves receive from God." (2 Corinthians 1:3-4)

Not only is the Lord the "father," the very progenitor, of compassion, but He is the God of *all* comfort. Synonyms for "comfort" include consolation, solace, condolence, sympathy, and commiseration—and God provides all of those, and more. Often, the physical illustrates the spiritual. Think, for example, of a little boy who falls and hurts himself. He'll get up and look for his mother, and as soon as he spots her, he'll wail in agony. Usually, what happens next is that the mother will take the boy in her arms, talk to him with a soothing baby voice, and kiss him where it hurts. The transformation is miraculous. The boy stops crying and, almost instantly, feels better. He's been comforted, and the mother continues her comforting as she tends to the wound.

> Not only is the Lord the "father,"
> the very progenitor, of compassion,
> but He is the God of ALL comfort.

In the same way, God wants to attend to our wounds, but first He desires to bring comfort. In Mark 1, we read of a man with leprosy who came to Jesus and begged Him on his knees, "If you are willing, you can make me clean." It's understandable the leper would ask Christ if He was willing; in his life experience as an untouchable outcast, he surely doubted anyone was willing to help him. Jesus responded in glorious compassion and comfort. Christ "reached out his hand and touched the man. 'I am willing,' he said. 'Be clean!' Immediately the leprosy left him and he was cleansed." (Mark 1:41b-42) In comfort, Jesus caressed the leper; in compassion, He healed him.

God longs to do the same for us. He is entirely capable of comforting us *in* and *through* any type of pain or suffering. But it's hard to see that when we are being hurt. Before I was born, my mother was a Roman Catholic and my father was an Episcopalian. They eloped, but my mother wanted a church wedding, so the bishop of the Roman Catholic diocese gave them a special dispensation that allowed for a church wedding so long as their children were raised Catholic. My mother was twenty when she had me, the firstborn of four. While I was a little boy, my father first worked as a cattle rancher on my grandfather's ranch in northern Arizona. When he decided there was no future in that business, we moved back to Tucson where he worked a full-time job while attending classes full-time. Three-and-a-half years later, he earned his degree in mechanical engineering. He was a motivated man, and his philosophy of life was that if you don't like your situation, you should do something to change it. That mindset kept us on the move throughout my upbringing. My parents had been married thirty-three years when my mother died of cancer, and in that time we had moved thirty-seven times.

So when I started eighth grade, I was coming into my ninth different school. I was a small, skinny kid, all of four-foot-six and eighty pounds. When I walked into class on my first day of school, a tall, burly eighth grader looked at me and sneered. "Hey, kid. Third grade is down the hall."

And that was just the beginning. The year was 1964 and The Beatles had come to America. Everyone was getting the Mop Top, the distinctive haircut of the Fab Four, but my father gave me a buzz cut once every four weeks whether I needed it or not. Add in that my last name is "O'Hair," and you don't need much of an imagination to know what eighth graders did with that. My nicknames ranged from the logical "No Hair O'Hair" and "O'Hairless" to the illogical "Hairy Ape." But every one of them stung. Then came the indignity of physical education class in the basketball gym where, because of my size and lack of athletic prowess (I had to concentrate so hard on dribbling that opponents would simply yell at me and I'd lose the ball), I was not only the last one picked, but the chosen captains actually argued over which one of them was going to be forced to have me on their team.

It was an extremely painful year—so I made a decision. I chose to deal with my hurt not by trusting in God, but by trusting in myself. I developed an image and came up with a strategy to protect myself from the pain being inflicted upon me. I based my image on a character from the Warner Brothers cartoons featuring Foghorn Leghorn. You may remember how this laughable rooster with the Southern drawl sought to woo the widowed hen Miss Prissy. Her bookish son, Egghead Jr., had an oversized cranium, wore glasses, and was smart. Foghorn did his best to try to show Egghead Jr. how to be a real boy, but the wee chicken was far too much of a brainiac for Foghorn's adventuresome antics. It was in Egghead Jr. that I found a view of myself. Like Egghead Jr., I had skinny chicken legs and was in my head a lot, and I also thought I could be funny just like the cartoon.

With Egghead Jr. as my internal template, I then acted to offset a personality trait that had dominated my childhood. My mother kept all of my elementary school report cards, and the teacher comments on most of the cards expressed that I was a quiet kid. In the eighth grade, I decided I was going to give up being quiet. I began preempting the verbal assaults about my size and haircut through self-deprecating humor. "Oh, you don't want to pick me for the team," I told the arguing captains in P.E. "I'm not going to help your team at all." Or I'd say, "Hey, I like the butch haircut. It's good for me. After all, it's easy to clean, and I don't have to waste time drying my hair." I found that this outgoing, humorous approach disarmed the attacks before they were launched, helped to cut the tension, and most of all, put me in control of the situation.

Pain and shame have incredible power,
and they certainly did in my life as
a child and youngster.

Throughout my high school years, I also pursued sports where I could at least be involved. As a freshman at a large high school in California, I was the fifth-string cornerback on the "C" team, a squad made up of small boys. I played all of two downs the entire season, but I was on the team. I played tennis there, too, and actually made the same squad from which one teammate went on to play professionally. The next two years overseas I developed soccer skills that, upon my return to the States for my senior year, made me more competent than most of the other players. But my tour de force was O'Hair's Hellions, a cheer group that went to the football and basketball games. We had no trouble getting the crowd going with our enthusiasm and our humor-laced chants against the other team. We were clever and beloved by our school's fan base, and it further supported the image I had created for myself.

The tragedy of it all was that, even though I was a Catholic then and had knowledge of God, I did not seek to trust Him. Instead, I did everything I could to lessen the sting of the pain I'd endured as a boy who was the brunt of the jokes and the target of the teasing. Brennan Manning, author of *The Ragamuffin Gospel*, described what I was doing as hiding behind the mask. My disguise presented me as a humorous, competent person impervious to hurt, but inside I was afraid from my pain and terrified about what was going to happen if I was unmasked and revealed for who I thought I really was.

A trio of incidents, each three years apart, were instrumental in shaping my self-image. In third grade, a neighborhood boy and I decided to have a fight, not because we were angry with each other, but just to have a nice scuffle. We started sparring, prancing about and jabbing but never landing a punch. At one point, I backed away from a swing, tripped over my own feet, and fell backwards. As the boy rushed me, I conjured up a scene from a western I'd watched where the prone cowboy, confronted by an attacking Indian, put up his leg and flipped him over. I tried the surefire move—only to watch the boy grab my foot and proceed to drag me around in circles. In my failure, I was ashamed and immediately thought, "I don't know how to fight."

Then, in sixth grade, I was in a park by myself on a Saturday morning. I saw a girl on the merry-go-round, and went up to her and asked if I could get on, too. She agreed and I started moving the apparatus in a circle, but only at a snail's pace. "Is it okay if I go faster?" I asked. "Sure," she said, so I quickened the pace for a few revolutions more before she asked if she could get off. I stopped the merry-go-round, she departed, and we went our separate ways and played on some of the other equipment. About twenty minutes later, I was walking away from the playground when I was confronted by three other boys, all a few years older than me. We started talking, and then the largest of the three leaned toward me and I backed away—only to fall backwards over another boy who, unnoticed by me, had positioned himself behind me on all fours. One of them said, "We're gonna beat you up!"

Flat on the seat of my pants, I asked, "Why? What did I do?"

He responded, "You scared my little sister on the merry-go-round!"

Frightened, I didn't try to run away, but I kept my wits about me and explained that I didn't intend to scare her. My verbosity spared me from a beating, but they warned me never to play with the girl again. As they left, I sat up in shame and heard a voice inside say, "See? You can't fight."

Fast forward, then, to ninth grade, not long after I birthed my Egghead Jr. persona. I was walking alone in a big field near my home when two older boys came up to me.

"We want to play a game with you."

"Okay," I answered with as much bravado as I could muster. "What's the game?"

"Nimbly-peg." One of the boys then held out a six-inch hunting knife.

My heart raced. "I don't want to play this game."

"Too bad." He pointed the blade straight at me. It gleamed menacingly in the sunlight. "Here's what we're going to do. You're going to stand right there with your feet apart, and we're going to throw the knife in-between your feet. You can't move."

And you can't fight, my thoughts accused. I believed every word.

They slung the knife over and over between my feet for a good fifteen minutes before they got bored and left. After I stopped trembling, I went home and told my parents what happened. The two guys, ironically both Boy Scouts, were punished. But that didn't matter to me. All I knew was that I couldn't fight. I was a chicken, just like Egghead Jr. Not even my humor could save me that day from the humiliation and the shame it brought once more to the surface of my psyche.

My inner response to my childhood experiences and the façade I chose to create in eighth grade to protect myself from pain reflected the pattern we saw of Adam and Eve in Genesis: they were afraid because they were naked, so they hid. Pain and shame have incredible power, and they certainly did in my life as a child and youngster—but God wants us to trust Him instead of hide; to go to Him for comfort instead of try to take control. Other response patterns common to all human beings reveal themselves as we look at how temptation works. Remember in Genesis how Eve saw that the fruit was good for food, was pleasing to the eye, and was desirable for gaining wisdom? John says this in one of his epistles in the New Testament.

> "For everything in the world—the lust of the flesh, the lust of the eyes, and the pride of life—comes not from the Father but from the world." (1 John 2:16)

Eve's responses to the serpent's temptation about the fruit mirrored the three attributes listed in this verse, and they do not originate with God. The same three responses came into play when Satan tempted Jesus in the wilderness in Matthew 4:1-11. After fasting forty days and forty nights, Christ was hungry and Satan came to Him and said, "If you are the Son of God, tell these stones to become bread." This appealed to a lust of the flesh (hunger). But Jesus answered, "It is written: 'Man shall not live on bread alone, but on every word that comes from the mouth of God.'" Next Satan took Christ to Jerusalem and had Him stand on the highest point of the temple. "If you are the Son of God," he said, "throw yourself down. For it is written: '"He will command his angels concerning you, and they will lift you up in their hands, so that you will not strike your foot against a stone.'" This appealed to the pride of life (Christ's privileged position as God's Son). Yet Jesus answered, "It is also written: 'Do not put the Lord your God to the test.'" Finally, Satan took Christ to a high mountain and showed Him all the kingdoms of the world. "All this I will give you," he said, "if you will bow down and worship me."

This targeted a lust of the eyes (possession and prestige), not to mention Christ's very allegiance to His Father. But Jesus said, "Away from me, Satan! For it is written: 'Worship the Lord your God, and serve him only.'"

God knows how much we can take.

This account from the life of Jesus shows us that there is a proper, godly response to each of Satan's temptations—and to his words of accusation that he diabolically whispers to your mind. Paul adds this in his first letter to the members of the church of Corinth.

"No temptation has overtaken you except what is common to mankind. And God is faithful; he will not let you be tempted beyond what you can bear. But when you are tempted, he will also provide a way out so that you can endure it." (1 Corinthians 10:13)

There are three promises here that we can take to heart when we face choices resulting from our pain and shame. First, God knows how much we can take. Sure, we usually don't believe that in the midst of the trial or difficulty, but that doesn't make His promise any less true. Second, He will not let our situation proceed beyond the place where we often say, "I had no other way; the devil made me do it." No, we always have a choice. Third, with every temptation or circumstance, God will provide a way out.

When you are afraid and hurting, God says, "Fear not. I am with you. Trust in me. Let me comfort you. Allow me to heal your wounds." Yet the Lord will never override your free will. You must choose to trust Him and not yourself—and you *will* as you learn next to better recognize the common response patterns to pain and shame, and why those responses can be so destructive.

Chapter 4

SHAME

When my family and I were living and ministering in Kenya, a woman named Glenda, one of the staff members working with me in The Navigators' outreach to high school students, was driving through a slum area of Nairobi when disaster struck.

A ten-year-old child playing near the road ran unexpectedly into the side of Glenda's van. Hearing the impact and the child's cry, Glenda stopped the van, hopped out, and scurried to the back of the vehicle to discover the child lying in the road next to the rear wheel well, her leg obviously broken. In a panic, Glenda called me and I instructed her to immediately take the child to Kenyatta National Hospital, and that I'd meet them there. Glenda told the bystanders to tell the child's parents what had happened, and then she carefully picked up the child, carried her into the van, secured her in a seat, and drove to the hospital as fast as she could.

In normal circumstances, time is of the essence, but it was more so at Kenyatta, a government-operated hospital with a horrible reputation. By the time I arrived, Glenda and the child had been there for forty minutes and no one had attended to them. I went up to the desk and proceeded to create a scene, playing the role of the angry white foreigner, until the child was taken away for an x-ray. Afterward, with the child now on a gurney, Glenda and I were led into the very bowels of the hospital and were left in a dimly-lit hallway, a naked light bulb burning in every third fixture on the ceiling. The child had not been given any water, much less any medication for the pain. We were told to wait for the arrival of the orthopedic doctor. By the time he finally showed up, the child's leg had been broken for over two-and-a-half hours.

He had the x-ray in hand, and after introducing himself to us, he took the film out of the envelope and had me hold it up to one of the bulbs so he could view it. He then prodded the child's leg, causing her to wince in pain. "I'm going to need to set the bone," he said matter-of-factly. "Hold her down."

Right there, in the dank hallway and with no anesthesia, he grabbed the child's leg and pulled on the bone so he could realign it. The child screamed in agony. "Tell him to stop hurting me!" she shouted in Swahili. Once he had the leg set, he then took his thumb and rubbed and pressed up and down along the area to ensure the fractured bone was in the correct place. The child cried out with each probing touch of his hand. "If I don't set it properly," he pointed out, "I'll have to re-break it." Gratefully, he apparently got it right, because he then proceeded to plaster the leg. When he was done, we returned the girl to her home.

When it comes to the pain and shame caused by sin, we

tend to think that the wound will just mysteriously disappear over time. Yet this harrowing story illustrates that the old saying that "time heals all wounds" is simply not true. God points out how we tend to dismiss the wounds of others in His words to Jeremiah: "They dress the wound of my people as though it were not serious. 'Peace, peace' they say, when there is no peace." (Jeremiah 6:14) Even though the human body has a wonderful capacity for healing, the wound still must be dealt with in order for healing to be possible. We cannot leave a wound unattended.

> When it comes to the pain and shame caused by sin, we tend to think that the wound will just mysteriously disappear over time.

I think of a scene from the movie *Braveheart*, which depicts the tale of legendary thirteenth century Scottish hero William Wallace and his efforts to rally the Scots against the English king. As a battle began, an old Scottish father lifted up the gate of a fort so Wallace's fighters could go inside. As the man held the gate, an archer shot him in the shoulder, and the barbed arrow pierced deep into flesh and muscle, but the old man didn't let go of the gate. Finally, when all the Scots were inside, the man let go of the gate, broke off the shaft of the arrow, and joined in the fighting. Later that evening, he sat at the campfire with the men as they proceeded to get him quite drunk at the same time they heated up an iron in the fire. Why? They were getting ready to attend to his wound.

They knew the copious amounts of Scotch was going to help him endure the searing pain when they pushed the remaining shaft and arrow through his shoulder and out of his back, and then stuck the red-hot iron into the wound to cauterize it to stem the bleeding and prevent gangrene. Funny thing was, no one wanted to be the guy that shoved the iron into the wound. They passed the iron from one to another, each person afraid that the old man was going to slug him in the face despite his inebriation.

That, sadly, happens to us, too. When we see someone in pain, we don't want to be the person to step in and deal with the wound. We don't want to get involved or get hurt ourselves. In the motion picture *The Spitfire Grill*, a young girl travels to a town in Maine looking for a new beginning after being released from prison. She finds a job at the restaurant owned by an older, cantankerous woman who has a terrible fall and hurts her leg. As the girl placed ointment on the woman's leg wound, the girl asked, "Do you suppose that the healing of a wound is as painful as the wound itself?"

It's an amazing question, isn't it? All of us get wounded or know someone who is wounded, yet we don't want to go through the pain to help them get well or to experience healing ourselves. Hebrews 12:15 tells us, "See to it that no one falls short of the grace of God and that no bitter root grows up to cause trouble and to defile many." (Hebrews 12:15) That bitterness is the spiritual equivalent of gangrene, and it can set in if we communicate to others, especially fellow believers, that there is no hope for healing. God will wipe away each tear, we often say, but not until the sweet by and by in Heaven.

Yet a degree of healing *can* occur in this life, and it should. But we must recognize and accept that the process will involve addressing the wound.

There are many ways we seek to protect ourselves and rely on our own tactics in dealing with pain and sin. The first is **denial**. In the movie farce *Monty Python and the Holy Grail*, King Arthur faces a dark knight who doesn't know when he's beaten. First, he loses an arm, then the other, and finally both of his legs. He's reduced to a torso, yet he proclaims, "It's just a flesh wound" and keeps fighting. It's ridiculous as to be out of the realm of possibility—yet that's exactly what denial is. As a high school headmaster, I see this all the time in kids from homes broken by divorce. I'll ask them how the divorce has affected them, and they'll say, "It was hard," but they'll never say it hurt them. They'll even add, "It was difficult, but it wasn't all that bad." That's denial. Denial is a way to take control of the pain. If it doesn't exist, it can't hurt us. But denial, of course, doesn't tend at all to the wound.

A second tactic is **negative shame**. Paul addressed this in the Bible when he wrote that "godly sorrow brings repentance that leads to salvation and leaves no regret, but worldly sorrow brings death." (2 Corinthians 7:10) Positive shame (godly sorrow) is the guilt we feel from doing something morally wrong. It's good and compels us to repent or forgive. But we use negative shame (worldly sorrow) as a tool to take control by *blaming ourselves* for the pain caused by sin. Kids from divorced families will say, "If I had just obeyed my mother and father, they would still be together." That's a lie. Those parents are moral agents with free will. The break-up is their issue, not the child's perceived disobedience. Yet the child is the recipient of the pain caused by the decisions of the divorced parents. Sadly, these young people will use this same strategy to deal with future pain caused by others who betray them such as a boyfriend or girlfriend or a trusted confidant.

Self-blame was in play when I developed my eighth-grade persona. My offensive strategy in dealing with my pain was to be humorous and outgoing; my defensive strategy was to blame myself for having a buzz cut and for being undersized and nonathletic—and this strategy remained active within me for years afterward. One night in Kenya, I was on my way home from a Bible study and worship service at a high school. It was about 9:30 p.m. and my route included driving down the only two-lane highway through the Kawangware slum on the outskirts of Nairobi. As I drove, I felt the left rear tire on the van going flat. *What am I going to do?* I thought. I knew that the area was not safe at night, but I was approaching the sole streetlight on the highway. *I'm going to quickly stop there,* I reasoned, *change the tire, and get out fast.* I pulled over and stopped the van.

There are many ways we seek to protect
ourselves and rely on our own tactics
in dealing with pain and sin.

I got out the jack and tire iron and elevated the van. For the moment, I left the spare in the vehicle. It was secured by a combination lock. As I started taking off the lug nuts, a matatu minibus pulled up next to me and six young men disembarked. The matatu left, but the guys didn't.

"You have a flat tire?" one of them said. It was more a statement than a question. "Let us help you."

My hands began to tremble. "Guys, thanks," I responded with as much bravado as I could muster. "I appreciate your desire to help, but I'll be able to—"

"Oh, no, no," he responded as another one of the men snatched the tire iron away from me and began unscrewing the lug nuts.

I stood upright and walked around the back of the van to where the spare was located. A sense of cold dread brought a tingling to my chest. Not only was I outnumbered, but now dispossessed of my tire iron, I was disarmed. Then I noticed that two of them had found my briefcase in the front seat and was getting ready to open it. A voice in my mind instantly accused, *You can't fight.*

I could've taken off in the opposite direction in hopes of outrunning the group, but I didn't. Instead, just like when I was with the boys in the park in sixth grade, I chose to confront the situation using words. I walked up to the guy holding my briefcase. "Listen. My Bible and a few papers are all that's inside. I'm not going to let you steal it. I'll give it to you."

He looked at me. He was angry. "Steal?" Then again, louder. "Steal?"

I never saw the punch coming. His fist struck just left of my nose.

It probably saved my life.

The contact moved my head and neck sharply to the

right—allowing the other's man's blow from behind using the tire iron to hit the top of my left shoulder instead of cracking my skull. In the split second it took my brain to register both strikes and their ramifications, I also heard the voice of God. "Fall down and pretend you're knocked out!" He instructed. I did as I was told.

I felt someone remove my shoes from my feet while another took my wallet from my back pocket. I soothed myself in the knowledge that it only contained my driver's license and a small amount of money, but nothing else of value. I heard the jingle as they took the van keys, and heard their curses as they realized the spare tire was locked in the back, meaning that they couldn't finish changing the tire and steal the van. Moments later, I listened to their footsteps recede toward the direction they had arrived in the matutu. I waited, perhaps longer than was actually needed, before I opened my eyes and woozily stood to my feet. I was proud of myself for taking the abuse and still remaining conscious. But I still was in the middle of Kawangware at night with no transportation. *Lord, what do I do now?*

Just then another matutu drove up, but I was anything but relieved. In the trauma of the moment, I couldn't help but wonder if the previous scene was simply going to repeat itself. However, this matutu was empty except for the driver. He asked me what had happened, and I told him I'd been mugged by six young men. "Yeah," the driver said, "I saw those guys just down the road. Do you want me to take you to the police station?"

"Yes," I said, "that would be nice," but even as I got into the minibus my fears remained. *What if he's not taking me to the police station? He could take me back to the men so they can finish what they started. Or he may take me someplace worse.* I took a breath and hoped the fresh intake of oxygen would settle my nerves. *God, I'm in your hands.* He started driving and engaged me in small talk. Before long, the driver revealed he was the cousin of my supervisor from The Navigators. My entire body slumped in relief and I bowed my head. *Oh God, thank you!* I knew then that I was safe. When he dropped me off at the station, I reported the crime (and later learned nothing was done about it, undoubtedly because of a bribe accepted from the perpetrators, a common practice there), then contacted The Navigators office. A staff member came with a new set of keys, we finished repairing the flat, and I headed home.

Guess what I did for the next ten days? I employed my longtime defensive strategy. It was now over twenty years later since eighth grade, and I still played the blame game. *You were stupid to stop. It was your fault you were almost killed.* I piled on the self-contempt instead of simply facing the pain that I'd been victimized. As I dealt with the incident, my wife decided to initiate her own confrontation—toward me. "John, you think this is your fault," she said lovingly. "You think that if you had done everything right, you wouldn't have been hurt. That's not true. You can do everything right and still be wounded. Jesus did everything right, didn't He? Yet He still experienced hurt."

Her words were life changing. They toppled over the first domino and helped me to start to recognize that my defensive strategy was wrong and had to be dealt with. It launched the process that allowed me to learn what I know today: when a person blames themselves for the pain caused by sin, there's no logic in it—but there's genius in it if the person wants to stay in control.

The third way we protect ourselves and handle our hurt is to **blame others**. In Western culture, we're quite familiar with the term "victim mentality," defined as a learned personality trait where we tend to regard ourselves as a victim of the negative actions of others—and to think, speak, and act as if that were the case. This mindset allows us to deal with our pain by meting it out; we fight fire with fire. We are consumed with an internal seething that permits us to give ourselves permission to do evil to others because of what they have done to us. Even more, there is a sense of power and liveliness that comes with this type of control. But living as a victim and blaming others never ends well.

Take the example of Jean Valjean from *Les Miserables*. He was thrown into prison for stealing a loaf of bread for his starving sister and her children, an unjust punishment for his actions. Escape attempts added time to his sentence, and he ended up being incarcerated for nineteen years before he was set free. When he was released, employers and others took advantage of Valjean's criminal record and treated him unfairly and harshly. He ultimately ended up at the home of someone he thinks is a parish priest, who welcomes Valjean into his home, feeds him, and gives him lodging for the night. However, Valjean's victim mentality compelled him to steal the priest's silverware. When the police captured Valjean, they returned him to the priest's home where Valjean learned that the priest is actually Bishop Myriel, who then pretended that he had actually given the silverware to Valjean and even asked him to take two valuable silver candlesticks as well. The police accepted this explanation and left, upon which Myriel told Valjean that his life had been purchased for God, and that he should use money from the silver to make an honest man of himself. Valjean realized, by blaming others for what had been done to him and acting out on those feelings through thievery, that he was no better than the people who originally harmed him.

> **Living as a victim and blaming others never ends well.**

Blaming others allows us to justify our sinful behavior. It's amazing to me that the vast majority of pedophiles—people who were often abused themselves as children—inflict the same repulsive behavior on others. You'd think the horrors they experienced when they were abused would keep them from even considering such behavior. But they choose to try to take control of their pain as a helpless victim by creating new helpless victims. A stunning biblical account of sexual abuse is found in 2 Samuel 13. It is there that we meet some of the children of King David. Common to that time and culture, David had offspring from multiple wives. His son Absalom and daughter Tamar were brother and sister from one mother; his son Amnon was birthed by a different mother. The story starts with the revelation that Amnon had fallen "in love" with his beautiful half-sister Tamar—but his definition of love was questionable at best.

"Amnon became so obsessed with his sister Tamar that he made himself ill. She was a virgin, and it seemed impossible for him to do anything to her. Now Amnon had an adviser named Jonadab son of Shimeah, David's brother. Jonadab was a very shrewd man. He asked Amnon, 'Why do you, the king's son, look so haggard morning after morning? Won't you tell me?' Amnon said to him, 'I'm in love with Tamar, my brother Absalom's sister.' 'Go to bed and pretend to be ill,' Jonadab said. 'When your father comes to see you, say to him, "I would like my sister Tamar to come and give me something to eat. Let her prepare the food in my sight so I may watch her and then eat it from her hand."'

"So Amnon lay down and pretended to be ill. When the king came to see him, Amnon said to him, 'I would like my sister Tamar to come and make some special bread in my sight, so I may eat from her hand.' David sent word to Tamar at the palace: 'Go to the house of your brother Amnon and prepare some food for him.' So Tamar went to the house of her brother Amnon, who was lying down. She took some dough, kneaded it, made the bread in his sight and baked it. Then she took the pan and served him the bread, but he refused to eat. 'Send everyone out of here,' Amnon said. So everyone left him. Then Amnon said to Tamar, 'Bring the food here into my bedroom so I may eat from your hand.' And Tamar took the bread she had prepared and brought it to her brother Amnon in his bedroom. But when she took it to him to eat, he grabbed her and said, 'Come to bed with me, my sister.'"

"'No, my brother!' she said to him. 'Don't force me! Such a thing should not be done in Israel! Don't do this wicked thing. What about me? Where could I get rid of my disgrace? And what about you? You would be like one of the wicked fools in Israel. Please speak to the king; he will not keep me from being married to you.'" (2 Samuel 13:2-13)

This is a fascinating revelation about David as a father; he is a dependent parent, willing to allow his children to do anything to stay in their good graces, and Tamar knows this. Even more remarkable, though, is the calm character shown here by Tamar. She is being sexually assaulted, yet even at this terrible moment, she is intelligent and tries to reason with her lust-filled half brother. Unfortunately, her pleas were ignored.

"But he refused to listen to her, and since he was stronger than she, he raped her. Then Amnon hated her with intense hatred. In fact, he hated her more than he had loved her. Amnon said to her, 'Get up and get out!' 'No!' she said to him. 'Sending me away would be a greater wrong than what you have already done to me.' But he refused to listen to her. He called his personal servant and said, 'Get this woman out of my sight and bolt the door after her.' So his servant put her out and bolted the door after her. She was wearing an ornate robe, for this was the kind of garment the virgin daughters of the king wore. Tamar put ashes on her head and tore the ornate robe she was wearing. She put her hands on her head and went away, weeping aloud as she went. Her brother Absalom said to her, 'Has that Amnon, your brother, been with you? Be quiet for now, my sister; he is your brother. Don't take this thing to heart.' And Tamar lived in her brother Absalom's house, a desolate woman." (2 Samuel 13:14-20)

Enter Absalom. Without being told anything, he knew what his brother had done and he tried to do what most of us do when confronted with someone who has been hurt. "Don't take this to heart" is the equivalent to, "It'll be okay." The motivation behind such a response is understandable, but in the end its nonsense. It's not okay; it'll never be okay. Yes, down the road, healing can come through Jesus Christ, but even healing doesn't make the offense "okay." Tamar certainly wasn't okay. She was desolate—devastated, ravaged, and ruined.

Absalom then takes news of the rape to his father. David was "furious" when faced with the painful news, but even more telling was the rest of his reaction: he did nothing. He didn't comfort Tamar; he didn't confront Amnon; he didn't take his pain to God. He was utterly passive. No wonder, then, that Absalom emulated his father's example, at least in part. He never said a word to Amnon, either—but he hated Amnon because he had disgraced his sister, and he bided his time.

"Two years later, when Absalom's sheepshearers were at Baal Hazor near the border of Ephraim, he invited all the king's sons to come there. Absalom went to the king and said, 'Your servant has had shearers come. Will the king and his attendants please join me?' 'No, my son,' the king replied. 'All of us should not go; we would only be a burden to you.' Although Absalom urged him, he still refused to go but gave him his blessing. Then Absalom said, 'If not, please let my brother Amnon come with us.' The king asked him, 'Why should he go with you?' But Absalom urged him, so he sent with him Amnon and the rest of the king's sons." (2 Samuel 13:23-27)

Absalom had it all planned out. He created a situation in the sheepshearers gathering where he already knew David wouldn't want to attend, and figured he could convince his father to send Amnon in his stead. Perhaps David was suspicious, but his tendency to acquiesce to his children held and he gave in to Absalom's wishes. The story then reached its sad and inevitable conclusion.

"Absalom ordered his men, 'Listen! When Amnon is in high spirits from drinking wine and I say to you, "Strike Amnon down," then kill him. Don't be afraid. Haven't I given you this order? Be strong and brave.' So Absalom's men did to Amnon what Absalom had ordered. Then all the king's sons got up, mounted their mules and fled. While they were on their way, the report came to David: 'Absalom has struck down all the king's sons; not one of them is left.' The king stood up, tore his clothes and lay down on the ground; and all his attendants stood by with their clothes torn. But Jonadab son of Shimeah, David's brother, said, 'My lord should not think that they killed all the princes; only Amnon is dead. This has been Absalom's express intention ever since the day Amnon raped his sister Tamar.'" (2 Samuel 13:28-32)

It's interesting that, through Jonadab's clarification, we discover that surely the entire palace was already aware of not only Amnon's rape of Tamar, but also that only Amnon was killed. Everyone knew about the dysfunction within David's family, and in graphic detail. But David's way of dealing with pain was denial; Absalom's way was in blaming others and then in taking revenge that permitted murder.

> Exhibiting rage makes it easier to live
> with pain because when we're angry,
> we take control by masking the pain.

The fourth method we use, **rage**, is an extension of blaming others—but the response is more external and obvious. "In your anger do not sin," directs Ephesians 4:26. "Do not let the sun go down while you are still angry." Proverbs 25:28 says, "Like a city whose walls are broken through is a person who lacks self-control." Rage removes those things which restrain us. Proverbs 18:3 adds that the wickedness of being sinned against brings contempt. Rage takes that contempt and places it not on me, but on other people. Rick Atkinson's Pulitzer Prize-winning book *An Army at Dawn: The War in North Africa, 1942-1943* related how the American Army needed to "learn to kill." The key was for a soldier to develop so much contempt for the enemy that he had no qualms to kill. When we rage, we show no hesitation to bring harm to another.

In addition, exhibiting rage makes it easier to live with pain because when we're angry, we take control by masking the pain. We often use rage to communicate to others to back off, much like an animal that bares its teeth when under threat. We discover that our rage will frighten others away and even prevent those who might want to help us from getting involved. Even worse, anger allows us the opportunity to seek vengeance and get even for the pain caused to us by another person. Alexandre Dumas' classic work of literature *The Man in the Iron Mask* tells the story of Philippe, the twin brother of King Louis XIV of France, who had been unjustly imprisoned from birth by his father and whose identity was concealed by an iron mask. Fueled by contempt, seething rage drove him to escape from the Bastille and seek vengeance on all who wronged him. Yet revenge is nothing more than the poison we brew to kill another that ends up harming us when we drink it. It ruins us. This is why Romans 12:19 says to "not take revenge, my dear friends, but leave room for God's wrath, for it is written: 'It is mine to avenge; I will repay,' says the Lord." Yet when we rage, we say, "No, I don't trust God to repay. I will do it. I will take the place of God."

Finally, the fifth way I believe we protect ourselves and handle our hurt is to try to **numb the pain**. When I was eleven I got my first pocket knife. I was so proud of it and couldn't wait to try it out by doing some carving. I asked my mother for a bar of Ivory soap, softer and easier to shape than wood for a beginner, and went to work. I had fashioned a pretty reasonable simile of a human face when I decided to auger a hole through the middle while holding the bar of soap in my left hand. Of course, the blade shot through the cake of soap and pierced my palm with a slit deep enough to warrant a trip to the hospital emergency room. The doctor examined me and then explained (this was back in 1962) that it would require no less than nine shots of novacane into different nerves in my hand to suture the cut, so he said it needed to be done without anesthesia. Being eleven, I didn't fully understand what that meant—until he put the first suture into my flesh and I pulled my hand away so violently that I made the wound larger. This required more stitches and the aid of several hospital staff holding my hand and arm in place until he was finished.

When we know we need stitches or worse, we desire to be medicated to numb the pain. But with emotional pain, we never want the hurt to come back, so we work tirelessly to deaden the wound through addictive behaviors. From abuse of prescription medications to the use of alcohol, illicit drugs, and the newest rage, medical marijuana, we select chemicals to dull the pain; or we develop more psychological addictions such as pornography or video games (especially those involving role play) that release pleasurable chemicals in our brain, and can actually rewrite how our brain works, to desensitize ourselves from the hurt done to us. Intuitively, we know these behaviors are a temporary solution at best, but we don't care. We go back to them again and again.

This type of emotional pain management is destructive to us and others. Defeating addiction often requires getting to the root source that prompted the behavior, but we may not actually learn that source until years later in therapy. Until then, whether we're conscious of it or not, we make an intentional, purposeful choice to numb our pain—and Satan uses this to place us in such bondage, we think we can never break free.

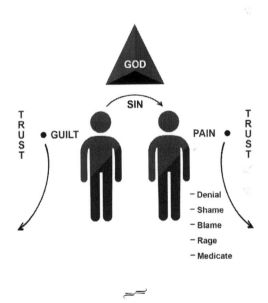

Here's a vital point to close this chapter. All of us who are victims and have been sinned against have a choice. We can trust God or we can trust ourselves. We naturally tend to do the latter, and our willful defiance to not trust God only exacerbates the problem. There is a popular movement in Christian circles today called Theophostic Prayer. It is a method used to help emotionally wounded people to acknowledge and identify the true source of their inner emotional pain and find lasting peace through receiving personalized truth *directly* from the Lord during prayer. Here's how it works. With the aid of a facilitator, the person looks at the sin done to them and then asks, "Lord, what do you have to say about this? Where were you, God, in the midst of this? How do you want to minister to me through this?" Then the person stays quiet and simply listens for a response from the Lord.

> All of us who are victims and have been
> sinned against have a choice.
> We can trust God or we can trust ourselves.

This is a positive and healthy movement, but I believe a key component missing many times from Theophostic Prayer is **repentance**. With this added element, the person also prays, "God, I acknowledge that I willfully chose to not trust you with my pain. I confess this now, repent of it, and ask you to forgive me for turning away from you." What does this accomplish? In addition to the confession of sin and the receipt of forgiveness, it allows the victim to understand that God was not absent or unaware when they were being sinned against. God was not powerless or unwilling to respond. He wept with us; He mourned with us. But it was done, remember, so that "we might not rely on ourselves but on God, who raises the dead." (2 Corinthians 1:9b)

The sovereign Lord, in His great kindness and mercy, continues to rescue us so that we might know Him more— even as we employ these same five methods to help us avoid the *guilt* of dealing with sin that, as agents, we commit against others.

Chapter 5

GUILT

According to *Time* magazine, Katherine Power, a student at Brandeis University in Boston, Massachusetts, was the leader of the radical National Student Strike Force in 1970. She and several others planned to rob a bank to get money to buy arms for the Black Panthers. Kathy drove the getaway car, but the robbery went awry and a police officer was shot and killed by one of Kathy's accomplices.

That night, Kathy began what would become a twenty-three-year life on the lam. Eventually Kathy moved to Oregon, assumed the name Alice Metzinger, settled down, started a new life in the restaurant business, bought a house, and got married and gave birth to a son. She became a positive, active member of her community and seemingly had every reason to be at peace. But by the time she turned forty-four, Kathy was desperately tired, chronically depressed, and tormented by guilt. In September 1993, she did the only thing she felt could do to end her agony—she turned herself in to the Boston police. She explained: "I am now learning to live with openness and truth rather than shame and hiddenness."

On the other side of the relational equation where one person sins against another, we have the agent. The person who sins against someone will experience a level of guilt for their moral failure. Sin and guilt are something from which we cannot run and cannot hide. Yet just like Adam and Eve, who tried to conceal themselves from God when they first realized they were naked and felt ashamed in their guilt (Genesis 3:7-8), we often try to run and hide instead of accepting responsibility for our actions and relinquishing control to God—the only one who can deliver us into wholeness and freedom. We experience guilt proportional to the severity of the sin we committed against others. That's why guilt can eat away at us even when we think we've successfully suppressed it or even left it behind for an entirely different life. Our guilt and shame must be addressed and confronted. Just like with our pain when we forsake God and trust ourselves to handle it, the approaches we use mirror the same five ways of dealing with our pain.

When we choose denial, it sometimes results in "the quick sorry."

When we choose **denial** as our way of dealing with sin/ guilt we have done to others, it sometimes results in what Larry Crabb calls "the quick sorry." This is when we say to the person we've sinned against, "*If* I've hurt you, I apologize," not "I *have* hurt you, and I'm sorry." We fail to acknowledge our responsibility for our actions, and instead give it mere lip service in order to deny the fullness of our guilt. If we do this enough, it can lead to a severe consequence: the searing of our conscience to the point where only a supernatural confrontation will make us confront our guilt. Let's return to that biblical hero with feet of clay, King David, to see how his denial of guilt from sins he committed played out in his life. In 2 Samuel 11, we learn that "in the spring, at the time when kings go off to war," David sent his men led by Joab and the rest of the Israelite army off to conquer the Ammonites. As they were away shedding blood, David was home relaxing. He decided one evening to take a stroll on the roof of his palace—and saw something he shouldn't have.

> "From the roof he saw a woman bathing. The woman was very beautiful, and David sent someone to find out about her. The man said, 'She is Bathsheba, the daughter of Eliam and the wife of Uriah the Hittite.' Then David sent messengers to get her. She came to him, and he slept with her. (Now she was purifying herself from her monthly uncleanness.) Then she went back home. The woman conceived and sent word to David, saying, 'I am pregnant.'" (2 Samuel 11:2b-5)

Not only did David defer from going into battle, he sexually took another man's wife for himself—and not just any man, but Uriah the Hittite, one of his best soldiers and later named among his thirty mightiest warriors (2 Samuel 23:39).

We can presume David was going to be content to keep his indiscretion a secret, but then her pregnancy forced his hand. He sent for Uriah and tried to get him to go home to his wife, presumably to have sexual relations with her so it would appear that he, not David, was the father of the child.

"But Uriah slept at the entrance to the palace with all his master's servants and did not go down to his house. David was told, 'Uriah did not go home.' So he asked Uriah, 'Haven't you just come from a military campaign? Why didn't you go home?' Uriah said to David, 'The ark and Israel and Judah are staying in tents, and my commander Joab and my lord's men are camped in the open country. How could I go to my house to eat and drink and make love to my wife? As surely as you live, I will not do such a thing!'" (2 Samuel 11:9-11)

Over the next two days, David entertained Uriah and even got him drunk, hoping the man would solve his problem by going to his lovely wife and doing what was natural. But even in his impairment, Uriah was a man of honor and a soldier who functioned the way David should've as king and commander but didn't: Uriah refused to go home. David's strategy changed from cover-up to hostile takeover. The next morning, the king wrote to Joab in a letter delivered by Uriah himself, "Put Uriah out in front where the fighting is fiercest. Then withdraw from him so he will be struck down and die." Joab did as he was commanded, but the battle did not go well for Israel. They lost many men because the fighting occurred too close to the city gates. Nevertheless, Uriah was still killed—and that was really all that mattered to David. "The sword devours one as well as another," David told Joab through a messenger. "Press the attack against the city and destroy it." When Bathsheba heard that her husband had been killed, David gave her time to mourn his death—then made his move. "After the time of mourning was over, David had her brought to his house, and she became his wife and bore him a son. But the thing David had done displeased the Lord." (2 Samuel 11:27)

The denial of our guilt can become so profound
that it can thwart and even exterminate
our ability to repent.

Incredible, isn't it? David ignored his responsibilities to his men and army, committed adultery, conspired to hide his actions, and when that didn't work, betrayed one of his most loyal men and had him killed at his command. That's a lot of sin with a commensurate level of guilt—and David did everything he could to deny it until God intervened through a prophet named Nathan.

"The Lord sent Nathan to David. When he came to him, he said, 'There were two men in a certain town, one rich and the other poor. The rich man had a very large number of sheep and cattle, but the poor man had nothing except one little ewe lamb he had bought. He raised it, and it grew up with him and his children.

It shared his food, drank from his cup and even slept in his arms. It was like a daughter to him. Now a traveler came to the rich man, but the rich man refrained from taking one of his own sheep or cattle to prepare a meal for the traveler who had come to him. Instead, he took the ewe lamb that belonged to the poor man and prepared it for the one who had come to him.'

David burned with anger against the man and said to Nathan, 'As surely as the Lord lives, the man who did this must die! He must pay for that lamb four times over, because he did such a thing and had no pity.'

Then Nathan said to David, 'You are the man! This is what the Lord, the God of Israel, says: "I anointed you king over Israel, and I delivered you from the hand of Saul. I gave your master's house to you, and your master's wives into your arms. I gave you all Israel and Judah. And if all this had been too little, I would have given you even more. Why did you despise the word of the Lord by doing what is evil in his eyes? You struck down Uriah the Hittite with the sword and took his wife to be your own. You killed him with the sword of the Ammonites. Now, therefore, the sword will never depart from your house, because you despised me and took the wife of Uriah the Hittite to be your own." This is what the Lord says: "Out of your own household I am going to bring calamity on you. Before your very eyes I will take your wives and give them to one who is close to you, and he will sleep with your wives in broad daylight. You did it in secret, but I will do this thing in broad daylight before all Israel.'"

Then David said to Nathan, 'I have sinned against the Lord.'

Nathan replied, 'The Lord has taken away your sin. You are not going to die. But because by doing this you have shown utter contempt for the Lord, the son born to you will die.'" (2 Samuel 12:1-14)

David denied his sin/guilt, but he couldn't hide it from God. The consequences of his sin were varied and harsh, and it's certainly no coincidence that the account of Amnon, Tamar, and Absalom detailed in the previous chapter happened shortly *after* these events. Another interesting note is that there is no record of David ever confessing the guilt of his sin to Bathsheba or to the family of Uriah the Hittite. Nor did he initially seek God's forgiveness. David *confessed* the sin once he was found out, but he never actively *sought* it until sometime later when he penned Psalm 51. The denial of our guilt can become so profound that it can thwart and even exterminate our ability to repent. No wonder Jesus teaches in Matthew 5:23-24, "Therefore, if you are offering your gift at the altar and there remember that your brother or sister has something against you, leave your gift there in front of the altar. First go and be reconciled to them; then come and offer your gift." Without confession and repentance to others we've harmed, our sacrifices to God will not be accepted.

Relying on ourselves to deal with the guilt/sin we have done to others through **negative shame** can be just as calamitous.

Why? This approach is based on the idea that we can deal with our sin—that we have the power to defeat and pay for it; all we have to do is show how sorry we are. This is our taking control. In 2 Corinthians 7:10, Paul reveals, "Godly sorrow brings repentance that leads to salvation and leaves no regret, but worldly sorrow brings death." Negative shame is worldly sorrow.

Self-flagellation is defined as the act of severely criticizing or punishing yourself, and it originated with the ritual of a person actually hitting oneself with a whip repeatedly as a method of religious discipline. As a young monk, Martin Luther was so beset by guilt that he engaged in self-flagellation, denied himself food, and allegedly tortured himself to the point of fainting. Yet he learned that these self-inflicted wounds did nothing to erase the guilt he felt; only the discovery that he was saved by God's grace through faith without works brought him peace—and led Luther to post the ninety-five theses onto the door of the Castle Church in Wittenberg, Germany in 1517, and launch the Reformation of the Christian church.

Of course, we Christians today tend to self-flagellate not with a whip, but with self-talk. We convince ourselves that our sin against someone else was so bad, so depraved or malicious, that God can't possibly forgive us. We limit His ability for our own sake, giving us control of our guilt because only we are therefore capable of forgiving ourselves. This is one of the most infernal lies Satan will tell us. 1 John 1:8-9 counters, "If we claim to be without sin, we deceive ourselves and the truth is not in us. If we confess our sins, he is faithful and just and will forgive us our sins and purify us from all unrighteousness."

The word "all" means just what it says. There is nothing God can't forgive. Even more, He is ready and willing to forgive us. Look again at David. After *all* he had done, the Lord took away his sin. His story from 2 Samuel 11-12 also teaches us that when we sin against others—people who themselves are the image bearers of the Lord—we sin against Him as well. This is why David wrote in Psalm 51 sometime after Nathan's confrontation, "Against you, you only, have I sinned and done what is evil in your sight; so you are right in your verdict and justified when you judge." (Psalm 51:4)

Deciding to **blame others** as a way of dealing with our sin/guilt allows us to justify ourselves and maintain control. Blame is a self-protective strategy to get others eyes off of us. When God asked Adam if he had eaten the fruit God had told him not to eat, Adam immediately blamed Eve and God himself for bringing Eve to Adam. "It's not my fault. My actions were the result of someone or something else." I remember an interview on *60 Minutes* with a convict on death row. He held up a convenience store and told the clerk, "Don't do anything dumb." When he discerned that the clerk was reaching to activate the silent alarm, he shot him dead—and in the interview blamed the clerk for obviously wanting to die because he foolishly tried to activate the alarm. In another case, the *Chicago Tribune* once reported about a hospital supply corporation that falsified its annual reports so that shareholders thought it was doing better financially than it really was. An auditing firm came in, but the company manipulated its inventory, moving the same goods to whatever warehouse the firm was inspecting. When the fraud was finally discovered, the corporation sued the auditing firm, blaming it for not catching them. The auditing firm eventually won the lawsuit, but it took eleven years.

Blaming others enables us to feel in control by trying to make the victim look to be the agent.

Blaming others enables us to feel in control by trying to make the victim look to be the agent. Hearken back to Chapter 1 and the Genesis accounts I shared. Adam said to God regarding Eve, "The woman you put here with me—she gave me some fruit from the tree, and I ate it." (Genesis 3:12) Yet recall that Adam was with Eve during her entire discourse with the serpent. I believe he heard every word that was spoken—but in this verse, he blamed both *her and God* for something he was just as responsible for happening. This is what we do all the time, and it shows how we trust ourselves. That shouldn't be.

Rage is a method of dealing with our guilt from sin we have done to others, and is an extension of blaming others, but with no control of our emotions. Rage justifies harming others verbally or physically and avoid taking responsibility for our sin. As with shame, anger here masks the guilt. We'll see instances of fits of rage played out every day in our courts. The common idea that if someone has failed at work or done something bad, they will then come home and kick the dog and yell at their spouse, shows this strategy of dealing with guilt on their terms.

The problem with rage is that it can feel enormously satisfying in the moment. Theologian Frederick Buechner wrote in *Wishful Thinking*, "Of the seven deadly sins, anger is possibly the most fun. To lick your wounds, to smack your lips over grievances long past, to roll over your tongue the prospect of bitter confrontations still to come, to savor to the last toothsome morsel both the pain you are given and the pain you are given back—in many ways it is a feast fit for a king. The chief drawback is that you are wolfing down yourself. The skeleton at the feast is you." In the end, allowing your guilt to justify your rage damages you as well as others.

Finally, we can resort to **numbing our sense of guilt** from sin we've committed against others by turning to chemical or psychological addictions in an attempt to distract and tranquilize away the guilt we feel. Oftentimes, people use marijuana and alcohol to numb the pain of their failures or sins. Through their high, they cover up the feelings of guilt and pain and don't have to face the damage they've done to others. It's like the person who says, "I drink to forget."

A friend of mine has a son who served in the United States Army in Afghanistan fighting the Taliban. This young man was as gung-ho as they come—born into a military family with a strong sense of patriotism and disdain for terrorists. He'd wanted to be a soldier for as long as he could remember. Once in Afghanistan, his company went on several search-and-destroy missions that involved trapping the enemy in an ambush and taking them out. However, the Taliban often used civilian women and children as shields. This young man took many lives in combat and knew some were civilians because he had to go confirm the kills. He did his duty in combat and fought against an evil enemy. He did nothing wrong; the evil of using innocent civilians as shields is the real evil here. Noncombatants are often killed in war. Killing someone who is not the enemy in an act like manslaughter still weighs on the soul and produces guilt. Not surprisingly, he returned home with Post Traumatic Stress Disorder along with a traumatic brain injury incurred during an attack on his company's base of operations.

> Only trusting God with our guilt through
> repentance and faith can place us
> on the pathway to wholeness.

What has he used to deal with the guilt he feels from the perceived sin of taking the lives of those who were not enemy combatants? He plays video games for hours on end. Oddly enough, Veterans Administration psychologists encouraged him to do so. Most of the games are fantasy or science fiction based but some, such as the Call of Duty series, strives to duplicate the actual situations he faced in war. My friend's son says the gaming reduces his stress and helps him control the frustration and depression he experiences because of what happened during his service. Its ongoing aftermath negatively affects his physical health and quality of living. He numbs his guilt as a way to survive a diminished life.

Sadly, that's just the result we'll have when we seek to avoid the feelings of our guilt of the sin we've done to other people—our lives will be diminished. Our wounds will not be dealt with and they will fester and worsen. No matter how hard we try to take control of our guilt, we know there's still something wrong. Only trusting God with our guilt through repentance and faith can place us on the pathway to wholeness. Remember the account of Judas Iscariot? Scripture tells us that when he saw that Jesus was condemned to death by the chief priests and the elders, "he was seized with remorse." (Matthew 27:3) Yet when he tried to return the thirty pieces of silver received for betraying "innocent blood," they replied, "What is that to us? That's your responsibility." (Matthew 27:4) Judas' shame over his guilt of sinning against Jesus led him to commit suicide; the chief priests and elders blamed others (specifically Judas) for the guilt of their sin against Christ, plus they didn't even place the thirty pieces of silver into the temple treasury because they knew it was "blood money." (Matthew 27:6) In this scene, there's plenty of guilt to go around and no one seeking God for forgiveness.

Juxtapose that, however, to the story of Peter and Jesus from John 21. We know that Peter denied knowing Christ three times prior to the crucifixion. Now Peter finds himself with Jesus again, the third time since His resurrection that Christ has appeared to His disciples. They are by the Sea of Galilee and have just finished having breakfast. Jesus said:

"Simon son of John, do you love me more than these?" "Yes, Lord," he said, "you know that I love you." Jesus said, "Feed my lambs."

Again Jesus said, "Simon son of John, do you love

me?" He answered, "Yes, Lord, you know that I love you." Jesus said, "Take care of my sheep."

The third time he said to him, "Simon son of John, do you love me?" Peter was hurt because Jesus asked him the third time, "Do you love me?" He said, "Lord, you know all things; you know that I love you."

Jesus said, "Feed my sheep. Very truly I tell you, when you were younger you dressed yourself and went where you wanted; but when you are old you will stretch out your hands, and someone else will dress you and lead you where you do not want to go." Jesus said this to indicate the kind of death by which Peter would glorify God. Then he said to him, "Follow me!" (John 21:15b-19)

I assert that at some point between Christ's death and this moment, Peter brought the guilt he felt from the sin he committed against Jesus to the Lord. He must've repented and received forgiveness, for why else would he feel hurt after Christ's third "Do you love me" query? "You know all things," Peter insisted. "You know that I love you." But that's not all. Jesus wants to make sure Peter knows that He *is* back in full relationship with Him. He tells Peter how He's eventually going to die for his faith—meaning that Peter, of course, was fully restored in faith and was going to be instrumental in God's plans for the future.

One of the greatest stories of repentance from the entire Bible is found in Luke 7. Jesus has visited an unidentified town and is asked by a Pharisee named Simon to eat at his home.

When a traveling rabbi spoke in a town synagogue, it was a Jewish custom for the local Pharisee to invite the visitor to dinner. Another facet of that custom allowed anyone who lived in the town to partake in the meal—anyone.

"A woman in that town who lived a sinful life learned that Jesus was eating at the Pharisee's house, so she came there with an alabaster jar of perfume. As she stood behind him at his feet weeping, she began to wet his feet with her tears. Then she wiped them with her hair, kissed them and poured perfume on them." (Luke 7:37-38)

The term "sinful life" seems innocuous here, but scholars understand that this woman was none other than the town prostitute. I speculate that she went to the synagogue earlier that day, heard Jesus' message of forgiveness, and was dramatically impacted by it—as evidenced by her actions. Imagine the scene. Each diner reclined on his side on cushions and faced the low-lying table, leaning on his left elbow so that his right arm was free to grab the food with his right hand. His legs and feet were behind him and away from the table. The woman came up behind Jesus, and her grief was so profound that she produced enough tears to soak His dirty feet. She then took the traditional covering off of her head, unfurled her long hair, and used the locks to wipe the muddied mix off of His feet. This must've made her hair tangled and filthy, but she clearly didn't care; significant, considering that her profession surely required her to maintain her beauty. She concluded by kissing

His feet and pouring the contents of the alabaster jar on them to purge the odor. It was a remarkably tender moment, but one person in particular didn't much appreciate it.

Our understanding of our forgiveness is directly proportional to our love for God.

"When the Pharisee who had invited him saw this, he said to himself, 'If this man were a prophet, he would know who is touching him and what kind of woman she is—that she is a sinner.'" (Luke 7:39)

Whether this was an inner musing or a comment Simon muttered under his breath to another person, Jesus heard it—and it prompted Him to ask His host a question.

"Two people owed money to a certain moneylender. One owed him five hundred denarii, and the other fifty. Neither of them had the money to pay him back, so he forgave the debts of both. Now which of them will love him more?' Simon replied, 'I suppose the one who had the bigger debt forgiven.'
'You have judged correctly,' Jesus said. Then he turned toward the woman and said to Simon, 'Do you see this woman? I came into your house. You did not give me any water for my feet, but she wet my feet with her tears and wiped them with her hair. You did

not give me a kiss, but this woman, from the time I entered, has not stopped kissing my feet. You did not put oil on my head, but she has poured perfume on my feet. Therefore, I tell you, her many sins have been forgiven—as her great love has shown. But whoever has been forgiven little loves little. Then Jesus said to her, 'Your sins are forgiven.'" (Luke 7:41-49)

Apparently, Simon didn't like what He heard Jesus say earlier at the synagogue, because he harbored such contempt for Christ that he failed to do the three things every good Jewish host is supposed to do for a guest: wash the feet, kiss the face, and anoint the head with oil. The Pharisee simply blew off these vital customs in a not-so-subtle snubbing of Jesus. As he was called to task for his actions, Christ also gave Simon an essential lesson about forgiveness—and closed by telling the woman that her sins were pardoned. Notable, too, is the fact that Jesus *faced* the woman as he corrected Simon and delivered His redemptive proclamation. It didn't matter to Him that she was the town prostitute or a woman. Jesus showed His esteem for her and His disdain for Simon's attitude.

His words also taught that the level of our understanding of our forgiveness is directly proportional to our love for God. The level of our love for God, therefore, is also proportional to our level of obedience to Him (John 14:21). Both managing our guilt and our efforts to deal with the shame of our sin indicate our level of willful defiance toward God. We trust ourselves instead of Him because we do not love Him the way that we should.

So what happens when we *do* choose to trust Him with our pain, shame and guilt? Thankfully, it's not something that we need to guess about or that He has hidden from us. It's fully revealed in His magnificent Word.

Chapter 6

TRUSTING GOD

Popular entertainment is filled with stories of people being brought back from the dead. In television fantasy and science fiction alone, there are the notable resurrections of characters Buffy Summers (Buffy the Vampire Slayer), Sam and Dean Winchester (Supernatural), and Rory Williams (Doctor Who). While these paranormal events may have been written into the storylines as much to revive viewership as anything else, they are nevertheless nothing more than trite fiction.

The Bible, however, tells real-life resurrection accounts dating from ancient days to the times of the early Christian church—and each one is superior to anything dreamed up by a screenwriter. Elijah raised a widow's son by stretching himself out on the child three times and calling out to God to return the boy's life to him (I Kings 17). Elisha used a similar approach to bring the Shunammite's son back to life after a head injury; he lay on the son twice before the son sneezed seven times and opened his eyes (II Kings 4). In Nain, Jesus saw a woman mourning her child as the boy was carried out of the town gate. He simply said, "Young man, I say to you, get up!" and the son sat up and started speaking (Luke 7). Christ raised the daughter of Jairus, the synagogue leader, even after He was laughed at for suggesting that the girl was "not dead but asleep." His command, nearly the same word-for-word as the one issued to the widow's son, caused the girl to stand up and walk around the room (Mark 5). Jesus raised His friend Lazarus even after decomposition had started because he had been dead for four days (John 11).

Peter—the very same man forgiven and restored by Christ on the shore of the Sea of Galilee—raised Tabitha from the dead after her corpse had been washed and placed in an upstairs room. He sent the mourning widows away, got on his knees in prayer, and then said, "Tabitha, get up." The woman opened her eyes, and seeing Peter, she sat up (Acts 9). Finally, there's the somewhat humorous resurrection account involving a rather long-winded Paul the apostle.

"On the first day of the week we came together to break bread. Paul spoke to the people and, because he intended to leave the next day, kept on talking until midnight. There were many lamps in the upstairs room where we were meeting. Seated in a window was a young man named Eutychus, who was sinking into a deep sleep as Paul talked on and on. When he was sound asleep, he fell to the ground from the third story and was picked up dead. Paul went down, threw himself on the young man and put his arms around him.

'Don't be alarmed,' he said. 'He's alive!' Then he went upstairs again and broke bread and ate. After talking until daylight, he left. The people took the young man home alive and were greatly comforted." (Acts 20:7-12)

Of course, the greatest resurrection of all was when God the Father raised His Son Jesus from the dead, "freeing him from the agony of death, because it was impossible for death to keep its hold on him." (Acts 2:24)

This is important when we look back on the verse from Paul in 2 Corinthians 1:9. "This happened that we might not rely on ourselves but on God, who raises the dead." The God who sees all things is the same God who raises the dead. When I go through painful circumstances, God permits it so that I will not trust myself, but rely on Him who has the power to raise the dead. Scripture reminds us that we will not always understand God's ways, but He has a sovereign purpose to draw us to Him through everything that happens to us. Life is given by Him, preserved by Him, taken away by Him, and restored by Him— and it's these truths that should compel us to choose to turn to Him instead of to ourselves when facing our pain, including the hurt caused by sin committed against us. But where do we start?

God has a sovereign purpose to draw us to Him through everything that happens to us.

The first step in moving to trust God with our pain is to **go to the Lord and clearly state to Him our recognition that**

we *are* in pain. It takes a direct, conscious effort to say, "I'm not going to rely on myself, but I have come to you, God, with my pain, knowing that you and you alone have the ability and power to tend to my wounds." This emphatically expresses, "You have the power to raise the dead, so you are imminently capable of dealing with my pain."

The physical illustrates the spiritual so well. When a child falls and hurts herself at the playground, the first thing she does is cry. When we're aware of our pain, it is normal and natural to cry. It doesn't have to express itself physically; it could just as easily be an internal weeping. After the child cries, she then seeks out her mother or father. I've often seen a child even try to hold in her cries, little lips quivering, until the moment she sees her parent. Only then does she burst out in tears. Our compassionate Father longs for us to come to Him in our pain with our wounds. Yet how often do we *not* go to God with our pain? We're not about to move toward Him. Why is that? It's because we see Him the wrong way. We think the Lord is in Heaven with His arms crossed and wagging His finger at us. No. He is the God of all compassion. We may not see Him that way, but our perception doesn't change the reality that He loves us dearly and He desperately wants to deal with our pain.

When the child reaches her mother or father, she eagerly accepts their gentle kisses or hugs of comfort. She stays as long as she feels the need to fully experience the pain and accept the consolation, and then she returns to her playmates. In the same way, we should allow ourselves to sit with God in our pain instead of trying to avoid it at all costs because we see no redeeming value in the pain. God wants us to sit with Him, resting in His presence and comfort and letting Him look on us with His gaze of love and compassion and touch us deeply with His truth. Pain is a tremendous teacher. There is much to be gained both in personal growth and in our ability to sympathize with others who are in pain. If our whole approach is to avoid pain, it's impossible to develop true empathy toward someone else.

In the Bible, a remarkable man named Job gives us an incredible example of someone who was determined to sit in his pain as long as was necessary. Job is perhaps the ultimate case study of someone who had to navigate unspeakable suffering and sorrow. A read-through of the entire book bearing his name is a must for every believer, but for now I'll provide a summary of Job's astonishing story. We meet him at his home in the land of Uz, a man "blameless and upright; he feared God and shunned evil." (Job 1:1) He may have been the wealthiest man on the planet. He had "seven sons and three daughters, and he owned seven thousand sheep, three thousand camels, five hundred yoke of oxen and five hundred donkeys, and had a large number of servants. He was the greatest man among all the people of the East." (Job 1:2-3)

But Job had an enemy—the same one we do—and the enemy came to God with an accusation. Satan claimed Job feared the Lord only because of the "hedge" of protection placed around him. Should Job face difficulty, Satan implied, surely he'd curse the Lord. Therefore, God decided to set the record straight, allowing the devil authority over everything Job had, but not over the man himself. In a sweeping run of disaster, Job lost all of his animals, his servants, and even his sons and daughters—but not his faith in God. "Job got up and tore his robe and shaved his head. He then fell to the ground in worship and said: "Naked I came from my mother's womb, and naked I will depart. The Lord gave and the Lord has taken away; may the name of the Lord be praised.' In all this, Job did not sin by charging God with wrongdoing." (Job 1:20-22) Job did not blame God. He mourned and, amazingly, worshipped Him. How many of us could do the same in the face of such heart-wrenching loss?

But Satan wasn't satisfied. He approached God a second time with a new indictment against upright Job. If the man is struck physically, Satan said, he will then curse you. Yet when Job was afflicted with sores from head to toe, he still trusted God. Job's wife, on the other hand, had seen enough. "His wife said to him, 'Are you still maintaining your integrity? Curse God and die!' He replied, 'You are talking like a foolish woman. Shall we accept good from God, and not trouble?' In all this, Job did not sin in what he said." (Job 2:9-10) Note that Job never denied his pain. He recognized it, accepted it, and took it to God.

That's when Eliphaz the Temanite, Bildad the Shuhite ,and Zophar the Naamathite—identified as Job's three friends— arrived. For seven days and seven nights they didn't say a word to him because his suffering was so great. After that, they tried to console him at first, but soon they began to blame Job for his own troubles, reasoning that he must have sinned in order for all of these trials to have come upon him. Job knew that this was not the case and tried to justify himself against their accusations. Time and again, he defended himself and God in spite of often being discouraged by these "friendly" discourses.

Nevertheless, as his pain persisted, like a fire bringing the impurities to the surface, Job began to question God. He expressed doubts he didn't know he had, and even began to wonder if God was actually aware of what was happening to him. "I say to God: Do not declare me guilty, but tell me what charges you have against me," he said in Job 10:2. "But I desire to speak to the Almighty," he added in Job 13:3, "and to argue my case with God." In Job 23:3-5, he lamented of God: "If only I knew where to find him; if only I could go to his dwelling! I would state my case before him and fill my mouth with arguments. I would find out what he would answer me, and consider what he would say to me."

Ultimately, the Lord answered in Job 38-41. God's response reminded him—and us—that He is sovereign and doesn't have to give us all, or any, of the answers we seek. "Who is this that obscures my plans with words without knowledge?" God asked in Job 38:2, and then proceeded to ask several questions of Job. "Where were you when I laid the earth's foundation?" (Job 38:4a); "Have you journeyed to the springs of the sea or walked in the recesses of the deep?" (Job 38:16); "Can you pull in Leviathan with a fishhook or tie down its tongue with a rope?" (Job 41:1)

Job responded, "I am unworthy—how can I reply to you? I put my hand over my mouth. I spoke once, but I have no answer—twice, but I will say no more." (Job 40:4-5) The Lord replied once more: "Would you discredit my justice?" He asked. "Would you condemn me to justify yourself?" (Job

40:8). In the end, Job concluded, "I know that you can do all things; no purpose of yours can be thwarted ... My ear had heard of you, but now my eyes have seen you. Therefore I despise myself and repent in dust and ashes." (Job 42:2, 5-6)

Our compassionate Father longs for us to come to Him in our pain with our wounds.

God used the pain to refine Job and bring him to a place of repentance. This is His goal for each of us in our pain. Then the Lord comforted Job with both His presence and restoration. "The Lord blessed the latter part of Job's life more than the former part. He had fourteen thousand sheep, six thousand camels, a thousand yoke of oxen and a thousand donkeys. And he also had seven sons and three daughters. The first daughter he named Jemimah, the second Keziah and the third Keren-Happuch. Nowhere in all the land were there found women as beautiful as Job's daughters, and their father granted them an inheritance along with their brothers. After this, Job lived a hundred and forty years; he saw his children and their children to the fourth generation. And so Job died, an old man and full of years." (Job 42:12-17)

God ministered to Job as he endured much suffering—and He will do the same for us as we trust Him with our pain. This second step in trusting God with pain is to **sit in our pain and** *allow* **God to minister to us as we** *join Him* **in His sufferings.** Like Job, we are to endure through the suffering and sit with God, wait for God, and experience God in the midst of it. As

Philippians 1:29 affirms, "For it has been granted to you on behalf of Christ not only to believe in him, but also to suffer for him." Did you catch that? Suffering has been *granted* to us in the same way faith has. Christ is God's gift in our suffering. This is not a verse many Christians put on their memorization list; suffering in life is not an option, but suffering with Christ brings deep meaning and intimacy with Him.

Here's the good news. God is with you in the sadness and suffering. As you sit in the pain, He is right there beside you, whether you feel Him or not. Hebrews 4:15-16 teaches us, "For we do not have a high priest who is unable to empathize with our weaknesses, but we have one who has been tempted in every way, just as we are—yet he did not sin. Let us then approach God's throne of grace with confidence, so that we may receive mercy and find grace to help us in our time of need." Later, the writer of Hebrews adds this exhortation.

"Fixing our eyes on Jesus, the pioneer and perfecter of faith. For the joy set before him he endured the cross, scorning its shame, and sat down at the right hand of the throne of God. Consider him who endured such opposition from sinners, so that you will not grow weary and lose heart." (Hebrews 12:2-3)

There are some rules of engagement we must follow in this second step in the process. First, we must trust God Himself, then trust that God will deal with our pain, but likely not on the timeline we wish. We are double-minded to love God and our relief. He is to be our "one thing." As the Great

Physician, the Lord knows what needs to be done and how long it will take. We must be patient. In addition, we cannot make demands upon God as we endure. Job learned this. He started well, didn't he? Yet as time ticked on, he started telling the Lord what he was going to say—and what God was going to do—and that never ends well. When we're in the middle of our suffering, we often try to wrest back control from God and have Him do things on our terms. We do this because we hate the pain, yet pain is God's invitation to wean us from trusting ourselves. God is good, faithful, and will never forsake us in our agony.

Faith endures the process—and it has nothing to do with how much faith you feel you have at the moment. Recall the story of Peter on the Sea of Galilee. Right after the miraculous feeding of the five thousand, Jesus told the disciples to get into the boat and go on ahead of Him to the other side of Galilee while He went up on a mountainside to pray. Later that night, the boat was far into the water and being buffeted by waves from a storm. So, shortly before dawn, Jesus went out to them, walking on the lake. When the disciples saw Him, they were terrified. They thought He was a ghost. But Jesus yelled, "Take courage! It is I. Don't be afraid." Then Peter made a bold decision.

> "'Lord, if it's you,' Peter replied, 'tell me to come to you on the water.' 'Come,' he said. Then Peter got down out of the boat, walked on the water and came toward Jesus. But when he saw the wind, he was afraid and, beginning to sink, he cried out, 'Lord, save me!'

Immediately Jesus reached out his hand and caught him. 'You of little faith,' he said, 'why did you doubt?'"
(Matthew 14:28-31)

Jesus' closing comment was not about the quantity of his faith, but the quality. The amount of Peter's belief was more than sufficient, but the *endurance of his faith* fell short. When he saw the wind, be became fearful—and it was only then that he began to sink. I believe that if Peter's faith had endured, he would've walked all the way to his Lord.

In contrast, look at the endurance of faith exhibited by that wonderful young Jewish trio in the book of Daniel— Shadrach, Meshach and Abednego. King Nebuchadnezzar made an idol and demanded that everyone in Babylon worship it when the music played. Anyone who defied this order would be thrown into a fiery furnace. When some astrologers saw that Shadrach, Meshach and Abednego did not comply, they went straight to the king to tattle-tell, and Nebuchadnezzar called the men before him.

"Nebuchadnezzar said to them, 'Is it true, Shadrach, Meshach and Abednego, that you do not serve my gods or worship the image of gold I have set up? Now when you hear the sound of the horn, flute, zither, lyre, harp, pipe and all kinds of music, if you are ready to fall down and worship the image I made, very good. But if you do not worship it, you will be thrown immediately into a blazing furnace. Then what god will be able to rescue you from my hand?' Shadrach, Meshach and Abednego replied to him, 'King Nebuchadnezzar, we do not need to defend ourselves before you in this matter. If we are thrown into the blazing furnace, the God we serve is able to deliver us from it, and he will deliver us from Your Majesty's hand. But even if he does not, we want you to know, Your Majesty, that we will not serve your gods or worship the image of gold you have set up.'" (Daniel 3:14-18)

The king was furious and ordered the heat of the furnace to be raised to seven times over its usual temperature. The three young men, faith enduring, were bound and cast into the furnace to face certain death. But that's not what happened.

"Then King Nebuchadnezzar leaped to his feet in amazement and asked his advisers, 'Weren't there three men that we tied up and threw into the fire?' They replied, 'Certainly, Your Majesty.' He said, 'Look! I see four men walking around in the fire, unbound and unharmed, and the fourth looks like a son of the gods.'" (Daniel 3:24-25)

Even in the fire, God was with them! And even in the fire, as the trio had declared, God delivered them! Significant, too, is that Shadrach, Meshach and Abednego were "unbound." In the heat of trial, they were set free—and so are we, if we endure and allow God to minister to us as He joins us in our pain.

This brings us to the glorious third step in the process, where we as victims then get **the opportunity to forgive**

those who have caused us pain by sinning against us. To do this, though, I believe we have to rethink, and even unlearn, how we go about practicing forgiveness—because most of us are doing it dead wrong.

> God is with you in the sadness
> and suffering.

In Christian circles, we have a tendency to adopt what has become an American proverb of living: to forgive and forget. When we're sinned against, we're not always keen on offering forgiveness, and even when we do, people often tell me, "Well, John, I forgave them for what they did, but I can't forget it. What's wrong with me?" I say, "Nothing is wrong with you—because God doesn't tell us to forgive and *forget*. He says only to forgive." Remember when Jesus appeared to Thomas and the other disciples in John 20. The Lord was raised from the dead and He was in His glorified body, yet what did He say in response to Thomas' doubts. "Put your finger here; see my hands. Reach out your hand and put it into my side. Stop doubting and believe." (John 20:27b) Even though Jesus had triumphed over death itself, what remained? The scars of the wounds. Every time Jesus looked at His hands or felt His side, He was *reminded* of the crucifixion and the pain it entailed.

So it's not a matter of forgetting what was done to us. We'll always remember. But we do need to forgive—and in the correct, biblical way, which requires three distinct actions.

Action #1: We are to ask *God* to forgive the other person, for *our* sake. Before we even consider forgiving someone ourselves, we first need to ask the Lord to forgive them. This is specifically modeled for us in Scripture.

> "When they came to the place called the Skull, they crucified him there, along with the criminals—one on his right, the other on his left. Jesus said, 'Father, forgive them, for they do not know what they are doing.' And they divided up his clothes by casting lots." (Luke 23:33-34)

> While they were stoning him, Stephen prayed, 'Lord Jesus, receive my spirit.' Then he fell on his knees and cried out, 'Lord, do not hold this sin against them.' When he had said this, he fell asleep." (Acts 7:59-60)

In both cases, it has been mistakenly believed that Jesus and Stephen were speaking these statements purely for the benefit of those who were there—to let them know they were forgiven. But that doesn't make any sense. The Roman centurions were simply carrying out orders at the crucifixion; the members of the Sanhedrin were responding to Stephen's perceived blasphemy. Neither group sought forgiveness or, arguably, would've even understood it in the contexts it was being presented. The truth is, Jesus and Stephen were speaking *only* to the Father and were saying what they were saying for their own sakes—to express their desire for God's forgiveness to be imparted to the others.

What are the other benefits of first asking God to forgive those who have sinned against us? One is that it is a natural continuation of allowing God to minister to our pain. Asking His forgiveness for the offender frees us from their power. In addition, it places us in the correct mindset. Many times, we think that the injustice done against us will not be properly served if we ask God to forgive the other person. But that line of thought simply doesn't fit with God's way of dealing with people. The reason Christ went to the cross and suffered horrendously was to take the penalty due to us (the victims) and them (the agents). When we ask God to forgive those who have sinned against us, it allows us to surrender our desire for vindication to Him, trusting that He is both able to give and to mete out justice in His way and timing.

Finally, first asking God to forgive will position us to be able to obey one of the hardest teachings of the Bible: "But if you do not forgive others their sins, your Father will not forgive your sins." (Matthew 6:15) Dr. Dan Allender, in his book *Healing the Wounded Heart*, told the story of a young woman who was sexually abused by her father. In Allender's counseling session with her, he presented her with an exercise on forgiveness. He told her to pretend the chair in which she was seated had two buttons, one on the left arm of the seat and the other on the right. If she pushed the button to her right, it would send her father straight to Hell; if she selected the other button, God would forgive him. For the next twenty minutes, the woman said nothing. She just looked to her left, then her right, then left again, and so on.

When she finally spoke, she said, "You have put me in a very hard place."

"How so?" Allender asked.

"If I push the button on the right, then I am no different than my father. But if I push the button on my left, then I have to deal with my pain as I ask God to forgive him."

The choice of forgiveness changes us, for it's through dealing with the pain and asking God to forgive that we are freed from the power and bitterness of the sin. It also shows our desire to see the mercy of God extended to the person who hurt us so he or she might be made whole.

> It's not a matter of forgetting what
> was done to us. We'll always remember.
> But we do need to forgive.

In his book *David and Goliath,* Malcolm Gladwell talks about forgiveness as he relates several stories from folks whose loved ones had been murdered. In one account, a family dealing with the loss of their daughter was visited by a stranger. He arrived the night the Derksen family of Winnipeg, Canada had learned of the murder of their daughter Candice. The stranger, a man in his fifties, told them that he, too, had lost a daughter to murder. He told how the perpetrator served a mere four years in prison before being exonerated by an appeals court. The man spoke of the three trials involved in his daughter's murder case and shared the information from a little black notebook in which he'd meticulously written every detail of the ordeal. He told of all the bills he had to pay, and how the process had destroyed his family and his health. He could no longer keep a job and inferred that his marriage was in shambles. "He didn't talk much about his daughter," Wilma Derkson said. "It was just this huge absorption with getting justice. We could see it. He didn't have to tell us. We could feel it." His constant refrain was, "I'm telling you this to let you know what lies ahead."

After the stranger left, the Derksons tried to get some sleep in preparation for their daughter's funeral the next day—and they thought about the man's tale of woe. By the time they spoke to the press, the Derksons had come to a decision. When asked how they felt about whoever it was who killed Candice, they said they wanted to know who it was so they could share "a love that seems to be missing" in their lives. They chose the path of forgiveness rather than destruction. By asking God to forgive those who have harmed us—in even the most heinous of ways—it actually saves us from further damage that can come as a result of the sin committed against us.

Lastly, when we are careful to seek God's forgiveness for others before doing anything else, it prevents us from foolishly going to the person first and saying, "I forgive you for what you've done to me." I see that as being nothing more than *moral one-upmanship* that is more about saying, "Look at what a good person I am. I forgive you, you worm," rather than having your expression of forgiveness come from a place of brokenness before God—that place that says, "I know all the things *I've* done wrong, Lord, and you have forgiven me. Now I ask you to forgive them for the sin done against me."

Action #2: Next, we are to *confront* the person who sinned against us. In Luke 17:3a, Jesus told His disciples, "If your brother or sister sins against you, rebuke them." Confrontation is vital, and it is done properly and with the right attitude when we have first asked God to forgive them. It gives us a heart of love and compassion, not of anger and bitterness. It also gives us vital perspective. Remember Joseph in Egypt when reunited with his brothers who tried to kill him? "You intended to harm me, but God intended it for good." (Genesis 50:20a) That's the mindset that allows us to rebuke out of a concern for the other person's well-being because we understand a bit of the bigger picture of what God is doing in their lives and ours.

I recall a time I received a needed rebuke. It was when I was in Kenya and I was visiting Scott, a missionary colleague who was serving with The Navigators in Tanzania. In the course of our conversation, I copped a snarky attitude and started going on about what I perceived as the various failings of pastors, saying things that were derogatory and unbecoming. I went on for about three minutes before Scott could take no more.

"John," he said softly but with authority. "Stop. Stop talking."

I did—and he continued.

"How are your comments helping to solve the problem? That does not reflect Christ well when you speak like that."

Ooooo, I thought. *He's right. My words are doing nothing. I've sinned. Lord, I forgive me, I repent.*

"Brother, thank you," I then responded. "You're absolutely right. My words have just continued to stir the problem, not help. Will you forgive me for sinning against you Scott, by what I've said? I will watch my words from now on."

He did forgive me, and since then I have worked (though not always succeeded) to check my tongue against words of criticism toward others. Scott's confrontation of me was done for my sake, not to put me in my place or shut me down, but to help me become a better person. That's always the end result of a rebuke delivered in the correct way and with the right heart before the Lord.

But confrontation alone is just the beginning. In His teaching to His disciples, Jesus then adds in Luke 17:3b, "And if they repent, forgive them," which leads to the third and most important action—forgiveness toward others.

Action #3: *If* they repent, we are to then forgive the other person *ourselves*, for *their* sake. You see, if we've followed the proper progression, we've asked God to forgive them and then we've confronted them so that now, IF they repent, we offer them our forgiveness for what they've done. This granting of our forgiveness is *conditional*. It is given *only* if the other person repents.

Consider the wife whose husband has had an affair. She has been betrayed and feels deep pain because of his sin—but she has gone to the Lord, stated to Him that she is in pain, and has sat in the pain and allowed God to minister to her as He joined her in that pain. As a result, she has accepted the opportunity to forgive her husband, first by asking God to forgive him and then by confronting him. Her husband, upon receiving her rebuke, is broken and repents—and not only says he will stop all such behavior, but agrees to go to counseling and be held accountable to her for his whereabouts when they are apart from now on.

All of this is good and she forgives him—but her granting of forgiveness *isn't a synonym for trust*. Forgiveness can be given if repentance is made, but trust must still be earned. If the husband, like the one in the illustration, is truly repentant, he'll do everything he can to earn back her trust over the course of time through his faithful behavior. This is what John the Baptist spoke of to the Pharisees and Sadducees when he exhorted them to "produce fruit in keeping with repentance." (John 3:8) True repentance produces actions. This is in line with Jesus' admonition from His Sermon on the Mount.

"If your right eye causes you to stumble, gouge it out and throw it away. It is better for you to lose one part of your body than for your whole body to be thrown into hell. And if your right hand causes you to stumble, cut it off and throw it away. It is better for you to lose one part of your body than for your whole body to go into hell." (Matthew 5:29-30)

We are to have personal ruthlessness in dealing with our sin—a determination that it will not happen again. When we lived in Kenya, there were no disposable diapers available at that time, so we used cloth diapers with pins. One day I was changing my son; he was not more than one year old. As I wrestled with the cloth, I pushed the pin through and harpooned my little guy right in his hip. I'll never forget the expression on his face. He was just gurgling along and then, all of a sudden, he looked at me as if to say, "What have you *done?*" I felt horrible and from that day forward always placed my hand between the diaper and his skin when changing him. I stabbed myself quite a few times, but that didn't matter. I saw what my careless behavior did to him.

**The easy yoke is better life
than suffering with bitterness.**

So what happens if the person who sinned against us refuses to repent? We should not declare our forgiveness to them. Remember, we've already asked God to forgive them. Our heart is in the right place and our conscience before the Lord is clear. We've confronted them as well, giving them the opportunity to repent and begin the process of restoration. We have done all we can as the person sinned against to have "compassion, kindness, humility, gentleness and patience," to "bear with each other and forgive one another if any of you has a grievance against someone" and "forgive as the Lord forgave you." (Colossians 3:12b-13) If they don't repent, granting them our forgiveness is nonsense—it's basically the same thing as telling them, "That's okay. You can sin against me again. No worries. Just bring it on!" Biblically, the unrepentant person is now at enmity with you, and Scripture directs you how to treat them going forward.

"Do not repay anyone evil for evil. Be careful to do what is right in the eyes of everyone. If it is possible, as far as it depends on you, live at peace with everyone. Do not take revenge, my dear friends, but leave room for God's wrath, for it is written: 'It is mine to avenge; I will repay,' says the Lord. On the contrary: 'If your enemy is hungry, feed him; if he is thirsty, give him something to drink. In doing this, you will heap burning coals on his head.' Do not be overcome by evil, but overcome evil with good." (Romans 12:17-21)

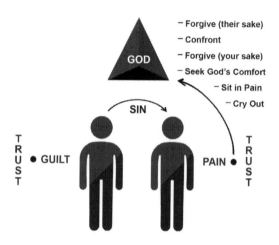

None of this is easy, I know, but the easy yoke is better life than suffering with bitterness. Turning to our powerful, risen Lord and trusting Him with the pain of being sinned against instead of going our own way is difficult. But we can be certain that the Bible is true when it says that "in all things God works for the good of those who love him, who have been called according to his purpose. For those God foreknew he also predestined to be conformed to the image of his Son, that he might be the firstborn among many brothers and sisters. And those he predestined, he also called; those he called, he also justified; those he justified, he also glorified. What, then, shall we say in response to these things? If God is for us, who can be against us? He who did not spare his own Son, but gave him up for us all—how will he not also, along with him, graciously give us all things?" (Romans 8:28b-32)

There is hope for us when we trust in God with our pain—and that same hope exists for us when we also trust Him with the guilt we feel for the sins we've committed against others. Let's discover how.

Chapter 7

HOPE

Workers for the Chicago Transit Authority have come up with some unique terms to describe life on the trains and tracks of the city. The elevated train often runs on a platform built above the streets, and in many places these platforms are quite narrow with just enough space for two trains to pass one another. As writer Anne Keegan described, if a workman was fixing the tracks when two trains came from different directions, he had no room to avoid being hit. Therefore, alongside the tracks a small platform only three feet square and projecting out over the street is built now and then—a place with a railing where workmen can escape. Workers affectionately dubbed these platforms "fool catchers."

As believers in Jesus, we sometimes play the fool. We lose our temper, bend the truth, neglect our responsibilities, or sometimes even do something criminal. We make decisions that in hindsight we realize were just plain stupid—and sinful against others. In these times, we need to remember that God has provided a "fool catcher" for us. It's called confession.

The first step in trusting God with the guilt for the sins we committed against someone else is to **go to the Lord and genuinely confess our sins *to Him*.** This requires us to admit what we did, without minimizing or denying anything, and taking full ownership of our responsibility for the sin. In *Child* magazine, writer Carolyn Hagan once wrote of a first-person account by Pulitzer Prize-winning author Alice Walker: "When I was a little girl, I accidentally broke a fruit jar. Several brothers and a sister were nearby who could've done it. But my father turned to me and asked, 'Did you break the jar, Alice?' Looking into his large, brown eyes, I knew he wanted me to tell the truth. I also knew he might punish me if I did. But the truth inside of me wanted badly to be expressed. 'I broke the jar,' I said. The love in his eyes rewarded and embraced me. Suddenly I felt an inner peace that I still recall with gratitude to this day."

In the same way, we find that confessing our sins to our Heavenly Father will allow us to see and experience His love for us and draw us closer to Him. Even more, God *wants* to receive our confession. Remember His words to Adam? "Where are you?" Recall His cry to Cain? "Where is your brother?" He desires us to come to Him in authentic confession. Upon confession, we move to a second step that is required in taking our guilt to God, one that none of us wish to do. **We need to sit in the damage of the sins we've committed against others to the point of brokenness.** This is different from sitting in the pain of sins done to us. There, God ministers to us as we wait on Him to join us in our pain. The outcome is that we partake in the sufferings of Christ as He meets and comforts us. When we sit in the damage of the sins we've committed, though, we allow ourselves to *see, feel, and experience* the hurt we've done to another person, oftentimes someone we deeply care for. This is far more difficult to do and is rarely actually attained.

> **Allow the victim of our actions to reflect to us the impact of our sin.**

A tendency I have observed in men who are abusive to their loved ones or who struggle with pornography addiction is that their sin is recurring. Guys will offer the "the quick sorry" I mentioned early in Chapter 5 and may assault themselves with negative shame, thinking that if they do this enough the sinful cycle will simply go away. Yet it never works because they are not sitting in the damage and becoming horrified at the damage they have done, and as a result, are broken by what they're doing to the other person and to themselves.

So how do we sit in the damage to the point of experiencing our brokenness? A good place to start as a Christian is to allow the victim of our actions to reflect to us the impact of our sin. Ask them how our actions affected them. Ask about how we hurt them. Then listen; do not deflect, defend or deny. Receive what they say. Do not jump to offering a quick sorry. It will be very uncomfortable to allow the weight of your actions to impact you. If you cannot get a response from the person you sinned against, ponder the passion of Christ. Picture in your mind the profound suffering Jesus endured—from sweating drops of blood in the Garden of Gethsemane, to the beatings and floggings inflicted by the Romans, to the nails being driven into His hands and feet and the spear thrust into His side—as He took on all of our sins and *made them His own* in order to be the only possible sacrifice to free us from the bondage of our sins. Now go even one step further and consider the shame He endured (Hebrews 12:2) as He took the emotional abuse hurled at Him during the crucifixion itself—and then juxtapose that with the shame of our own sins and the guilt it brings. Take time to realize that your actions did that to Christ. No, it is not possible to truly feel what Jesus felt, but it can provide a glimpse of what it's like to experience the damage of our sins.

I'll never forget how this happened with my wife Susie. We were studying Larry Crabb's insightful book *The Marriage Builder*, and did a communication exercise in which we reviewed a variety of interactions between a husband and a wife. One such dialogue read like this:

Husband: "At the Bible study last night, when I said what I thought the verse meant, you frowned and said, "Oh, I don't think it means that." I felt like walking out and never coming back. I'm still mad about it!"

Wife: "Oh honey, I'm so sorry, I really feel badly that I did that to you."

Susie and I then studied Crabb's comment on that interaction. "Apologies offered too quickly before you let your spouse know that you understand the feelings that were shared usually mean nothing. They really amount to the message, 'I don't want to discuss this further and I don't really want to hear how badly I hurt you.'"

I felt more than a twinge of conviction in my heart as I read that, and my guilt was affirmed when we read the dialogue as it should've been said.

Husband: "At the Bible study last night, when I said what I thought the verse meant, you frowned and said, "Oh, I don't think it means that." I felt like walking out and never coming back. I'm still mad about it!"

Wife: "I'm not sure I understand what made you feel so angry. Did you feel that I was putting you down?"

Crabb explained, "Listen carefully to what your spouse is saying. If you're not sure you really understand what is being expressed, explore what was meant by asking questions. Your partner will likely interpret this to mean that you really want to know what he or she felt."

I realized I was often like the wife in the first interaction. I offer "the quick sorry." So I asked Susie, "Do I do this to you?" She didn't hesitate. "Oh, yeah."

"Tell me what it's like for you when I say, 'I'm sorry.'"

Her response still brings me to fresh tears. "You don't see me. You're not really interested in me."

My heart was pierced. The impact of my unwillingness to sit in the damage of my sins committed against her went far beyond her feeling that I was not listening to her. For Susie, it was as if she wasn't there at all.

As I thought about her response in the days that followed, I remembered that Susie is the youngest of four daughters of a father who was a Navy SEAL. He never made a secret of the fact that he always wanted a son. As the last born, my wife keenly felt that. What must it have been like for her to be a girl when she knew her father really wanted a boy? Her father didn't see her for who she really was. No wonder she would respond similarly to me when I offered my quick sorry.

So I made a decision to stop saying "I'm sorry" when I sinned against my wife, but to instead allow myself to sit in the damage of what I had done. This was not easy. Just one example came the day I let my anger get out of control. We live in a home that does not have a sidewalk between the end of the front yard and the curb to the street. There is an eight-foot wide space there, but it is dirt. My neighbors on each side have mesquite trees that protrude from their yard and over-hang that eight-foot wide space in front of their homes so that no one could walk there if they wanted to. Therefore, folks simply trek on the side of the street when they walk in front of our home. I decided to better utilize the space by parking my car in it. I made this a routine that Susie saw and assumed it was acceptable.

Then came the afternoon I walked out to the car to find a traffic ticket wedged beneath the windshield wiper. It cited a violation for parking in the sidewalk and had a fine of nearly two-hundred dollars.

I was incensed! *This is wrong. This is unjust,* I fumed inter-nally. *Didn't Susie just drive the car this morning?* I marched inside the house and found her in the kitchen.

"You just got us a parking ticket!" I yelled.

She pivoted around and glared at me. "What are you talking about?"

I showed her the ticket. "See what you did?"

"What I did?" she said. "You park there all the time. I was

just doing what you've always done. Why are you blaming me?"

I realized at that moment that my anger should have been directed at the city bureaucrats who made such a stupid law of a parking violation over a sidewalk that didn't even exist. I looked at my wife. She was understandably angry and hurt. I wanted to say I was sorry. Instead, I said, "Suze, I have sinned against you. I have allowed my anger about the ticket to be taken out on you. That was wrong of me. How does it make you feel?"

She said, "It's like you don't value me. You don't hold me in esteem."

Repentance carries with it the idea that we are to stop, turn, and go in the opposite direction.

Once more, I allowed myself to sit in the damage of my sin and reflect on the harm I did to my wife because of my sin. I was broken—and that brokenness taught me how to then achieve the final step in trusting God with the guilt for the sins we commit against someone else: **repentance**. Repentance is different from confession. While confession is an admittance of wrongdoing where we take ownership of and responsibility for our sins, repentance carries with it the idea that we are to stop, turn, and go in the opposite direction. It is a renunciation of what we've thought or done.

How does this work? Now that we've confessed our sins to the Lord and have sat in the damage of our sins, we can ask ourselves, "What feeling can I touch inside me that was operating when I had this attitude or behavior?" We want to see the willful defiance of God and His commands behind our decision to sin. It is at this point that we **repent to God and seek His forgiveness.** "Lord, I repent. I want to turn away from that attitude or behavior, and I ask you to forgive me."

To put on the new self,
I had to put off my deceitful desires
by asking God to deal with my sin.

John Lynch talks about how Christians believe in sin management. We know we sin and we have been taught to confess our sins. We think we confess and it goes away. We have the power to move sin out of the way. The problem is that sin is far more powerful than our will and choices. We have *no* power over sin. God does forgive us our sins; He is faithful. The point here is that God alone has power over our sin; we have no power over it! Just as we need the comfort of the Lord in our pain, we need the power of God to free us from sin. Ephesians 4:17-24 says,

> "So I tell you this, and insist on it in the Lord, that you must no longer live as the Gentiles do, in the *futility of their thinking.* They are *darkened in their understanding* and separated from the life of God because of *the ignorance that is in them* due to the hardening of their hearts. Having lost all sensitivity, they have given

themselves over to sensuality so as to indulge in every kind of impurity, and they are full of greed.

That, however, is not the way of life you learned when you heard about Christ and were taught in him in accordance with the truth that is in Jesus. You were taught, with regard to your former way of life, to put off your old self, which is being *corrupted by its deceitful desires*; to be *made new in the attitude of your minds*; and *to put on the new self*, created to be like God in true righteousness and holiness."

The highlighted words in the first paragraph of the passage are the below the surface words describing our thoughts, attitudes and behaviors that lead us to sin. God is at work to transform us as those thoughts, attitudes and behaviors are brought into the light for God so He can work on them. That is how we show our trust in Him. The emphasized words in the second paragraph points out our old self is being corrupted by deceitful desires. What we want is hidden to us. We lie to ourselves and fool ourselves. God wants us to bring these deceitful desires to Him to be put to death.

How could I have "put on the new self" in my situation with Susie and the parking ticket? After I found the ticket and saw the fine, it was still appropriate for me to recognize the injustice. But when I became angry with Susie, it showed I had a deceitful desire and that my attitude was not right. This was an invitation from God to address my sinful desire to be seen as law abiding. I turned my anger on Susie and acted to protect myself at her expense. To put on the new self, I had to put off my deceitful desires by asking God to deal with my sin. Once that was done, I could then seek to know how God wanted me to behave. I could've made myself vulnerable and speak the truth in love like this:

"Susie," I say calmly as I walk into the kitchen. "Can you believe we just got a parking ticket?"

She turns around and looks at me. Her mouth falls open. "You're kidding me," she says in a disbelieving tone. "A ticket?"

"Yep, and it has a fine of almost two hundred dollars." I shake my head. "It's so sad that we live in a city that can punish us when all we're trying to do is something right to help our neighbors pass by our home more easily."

Susie sighs as her hands fall to her sides. "But I was the last one to park there this morning."

"I know, but who parked there isn't the issue; it's the injustice of it all." I toss the ticket onto the dining table. "This really upsets me, and I believe God is inviting me to trust Him with this injustice. I'm going to ask Him to tell me whether to challenge this in court or just pay the fine."

Had this occurred instead of what really happened, I would've avoided sinning against my wife and allowed God to deal with my deceitful desires in a way that benefitted us as a couple and brought glory to Him. This response of godly sorrow would've affirmed the biblical truth found in 1 Peter 2:19-21 that says "it is commendable if someone bears up under the pain of unjust suffering because they are conscious of God … But if you suffer for doing good and you endure it, this is commendable before God. To this you were called, because Christ suffered for you, leaving you an example, that you should follow in his steps."

In repentance, we put off our old, corrupted selves and deeply, not superficially, put on our new selves as image bearers of God created to have impact, significance, and to be loved well. This process first requires a transformation in our mind and heart, and then is followed through in our actions, resulting in a life that pleases the Lord.

"Therefore, I urge you, brothers and sisters, in view of God's mercy, to offer your bodies as a living sacrifice, holy and pleasing to God—this is your true and proper worship. Do not conform to the pattern of this world, but be transformed by the renewing of your mind. Then you will be able to test and approve what God's will is— his good, pleasing and perfect will." (Romans 12:1-2)

After we repent to God and seek His forgiveness, we then need to **repent to the person we've sinned against and seek his or her forgiveness.** After I confessed to Susie my sin of allowing my anger about the ticket to be taken out on her, found out how that made her feel, and sat in that damage, I was able to say to her, "Susie, I repent for my sin and for making you feel like I don't value you or hold you in esteem. I promise to do everything I can to change my attitude and my behavior so I don't get angry at you or blame you, and make you feel that way again." The onus is on us to repent, seek forgiveness, and then give God access to our inner life so deep, real transformation is in process. No, we likely won't be perfect in this, but if we employ this type of repentance / forgiveness response enough, we will build a habit of repentance and forgiveness that will see God dealing with our sin. It's two sides of the same coin: we trust in God on one side and stand against our own self-trust on the other. It's that combination of faith in Him and recognizing our power-lessness against sin that will ignite His power and prevent Satan from auguring us down in guilt.

In repentance, we put off our old,
corrupted selves and deeply, not superficially,
put on our new selves as image bearers of God.

There is sweetness in repentance and forgiveness. When we repent to the Lord and seek His forgiveness, we get to once more taste the kindness, mercy, and goodness of God first expressed to us on the day of our salvation. Yet when we repent of our sin against others and seek their forgiveness, we get to re-experience that same kindness, mercy, and goodness from another person. When this comes from a person we deeply care for, the taste can be rich indeed. I recall when my wife and I were meeting with our dear friends John and Patti Cepin for counseling using a broad-based, five-day training session modeled after Matthew 7:1-5 called "Potter's Wheel." In this model of soul care, we deal with issues in our lives through lessons learned looking back. Our youngest son joined us for one of the sessions—and he shared about a time that I had wounded him that was unrevealed to me until that moment.

It happened back when we were living in Kenya. Of course, Susie and I were there as missionaries, so we did our best to respect the Kenyan culture. One of its taboos was that husbands and wives never showed affection in public. Married people weren't even allowed to hold hands. Therefore, Susie and I followed suit in our behavior—and our son saw this and said he was in constant fear as a child that we were going to get a divorce. In fact, he believed that I didn't even love his mother. He lived with that despair for the decade or so that we were there, and being a child, he never told me what he was feeling. While kids are great observers, they're usually horrible interpreters; still, this did not justify my failure to ever offset his fear through my expressions of affection toward Susie when our family was in the privacy of our home. I could've done any number of things with Susie then: hold hands, hug, or give an appropriate kiss. But apparently I did none of those things, at least not to the point that our son noticed.

I was heartbroken to the point of tears by his revelation. I told my son, "Your interpretation of what you saw was not at all the reality in our lives. I loved your mother and still do. Yet I sinned against you. I want to repent of my lack of actions that caused you to believe your parents were going to get a divorce. I promise to do all I can to show you that I deeply love your mother. Will you forgive me?"

He responded, "Dad, I was wrong in my interpretation, but I want to forgive you."

At that moment, I felt the very mercy of God expressed to me through my son. The guilt I felt was replaced with the soothing balms of kindness, mercy, and goodness. The same thing happened when my other son told me of a time I sinned against him by not suspending or expelling from school some kids who had bullied him, even though I had the power to do so and had done just that on occasions of bullying involving other students. I was so focused on trying to teach my son how to stand up for himself that I completely overlooked the injustice done to him. He said it made him feel like I didn't care for him. Once again, I repented and asked for forgiveness— and when he gave it, God's mercy washed freshly over me.

> ### We deal with issues in our lives through lessons learned looking back.

I believe this is the greatest benefit of repenting and seeking forgiveness from another person. If they choose to forgive, the result is indescribably sweet. And if they decide not to grant forgiveness? We still have the healing that comes from God's forgiveness, which He always offers to the one whose heart is truly repentant.

Lastly, after seeking forgiveness, it is important to make amends. In the Old Testament it was called restitution. When John the Baptist told the Pharisees to bring forth the fruit of repentance, he was looking for this. When Jesus went to Zacchaeus's house, Zacchaeus told the Lord that he was returning ill-gotten gain and paying people back who he had cheated many times over. He was making amends for his sin. When we have confessed, sat in the damage, and repented, we are to follow that up with making things right with the person, bearing fruit in keeping with repentance. Ask yourself, "If someone sins against me in this manner, what can I do to make it right?"

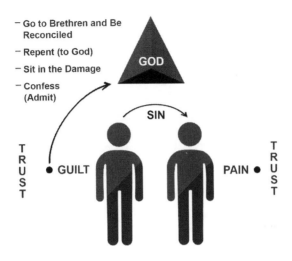

Confession, sitting in the damage, repentance, making amends, and forgiveness are the ways that we are able to experience and live out before others David's psalm of repentance from Psalm 51:10-13. "Create in me a pure heart, O God, and renew a steadfast spirit within me. Do not cast me from your presence or take your Holy Spirit from me. Restore to me the joy of your salvation and grant me a willing spirit, to sustain me. Then I will teach transgressors your ways, so that sinners will turn back to you." Remember, this is not a technique, not a specific order of action; it is a heart issue of coming to the Lord to deal with our guilt.

In both of my earlier statements of repentance, to Susie and also to my son, there was a word I could've used—but didn't. Let's look next at why I didn't use that word as we identify the first potential danger we must guard against as we accept God's invitation to trust Him with our pain and guilt.

Chapter 8

ACCUSER

I n the mythic structure of the storytelling in the *Star Wars* saga, an amazing truth emerges from what happens to the character Anakin Skywalker that has nothing to do with the tale's underlying Force lore. When he is a young Jedi in training, Anakin has nightmares in which he sees his mother Shmi, whom he voluntarily left when he was a small boy to begin his training, in mortal danger. Convinced they are a premonition of doom, he returns to his home planet of Tatooine to find his mother imprisoned by a clan of "sand people" called Tusken Raiders and tortured to the point of death. When she dies in his arms, Anakin goes on a rampage and kills every one of the sand people, including the women and children, in violation of Jedi code.

When he brings his mother's body home to be buried, he vows to the young woman who accompanied him to Tatooine, Senator Padme Amidala, that someday he "will be the most powerful Jedi ever. I promise you. I will even learn to stop people from dying." At his mother's graveside, Anakin additionally pledges that he will not fail again. This is where Anakin makes an oath he cannot keep.

Later in the saga, after he is secretly wed to Padme, Anakin starts having more nightmares, but this time he sees Padme dying in childbirth. He earlier made the oath to stop people from dying, and now believes his wife's life is in the balance. He confides in Sheev Palpatine, the supreme chancellor of the senate who also happened to be Darth Sidious, a dark lord of the Sith, the enemy of the Jedi. Palpatine had been slowly wooing Anakin toward the dark side, and tells Anakin the legend of Darth Plagueis, claiming that Plagueis had discovered a way to prevent death. Intrigued and tempted, Anakin asked where he can get this power. Palpatine responded, "Not from a Jedi."

> Our oaths made about things we cannot control can bind us to a very real dark force.

This set the stage for a final showdown when Anakin rescues Palpatine from Jedi master Mace Windu and chooses to submit to Darth Sidious, go over to the dark side, and become Sidious' apprentice. Sidious tells Anakin, "To cheat death is a power only one has achieved, but if we work together, I know we can discover the secret." He then renames Anakin as Darth Vader, and Anakin immediately plunges into deeper darkness to help his new master wipe out the Jedi. In the end, the commitment from Sidious to work with Anakin to stop people from dying was just a ruse. Padme loses her life in childbirth,

Anakin's journey to the dark side is completed—and the catalyst of it all was the oath over which he had no control.

Unlike the fictitious Anakin Skywalker, our oaths made about things we cannot control can bind us to a very real dark force: **Satan himself.** Defined as "enemy" or "adversary," Satan is an accuser of the believers in God (Zechariah 3:1; Revelation 12:10); in addition, Revelation 12:9 identifies him as the one "who leads the whole world astray." True to his character, Satan uses our oaths as a portal through which he tries to undermine our faith or even entrap us to bind us to evil based upon what we've said. Satan also always suggests ways we can regain control apart from God, because the accuser is ever vigilant to get us to trust in ourselves and our own limited abilities rather than to trust in God and His unlimited abilities.

One of the observed actions that takes place when we sin against another is how our commitment to be in control leads us to utter vows. In our pain or guilt, we have a tendency to say things to ourselves or others that we shouldn't. Back when God gave the law to the Jewish nation, He pointed out this sin. "If a person swears thoughtlessly with his lips to do evil or to do good, in whatever matter a man may speak thoughtlessly with an oath and it is hidden from him, and then he comes to know it, he will be guilty in one of these. So it shall be when he becomes guilty in one of these, that he shall confess that in which he has sinned." (Leviticus 5:4-5, NASB)

We add to our sin when we start uttering oaths. It is another sign that we are taking control of things we cannot control. Here are Christ's words regarding oaths from the Sermon on the Mount, followed by His brother James' elaboration on the same teaching.

> "You have heard that it was said to the people long ago, 'Do not break your oath, but fulfill to the Lord the vows you have made.' But I tell you, do not swear an oath at all: either by heaven, for it is God's throne; or by the earth, for it is his footstool; or by Jerusalem, for it is the city of the Great King. And do not swear by your head, for you cannot make even one hair white or black. All you need to say is simply 'Yes' or 'No'; anything beyond this comes from the evil one." (Matthew 5:33-37)

> "Above all, my brothers and sisters, do not swear—not by heaven or by earth or by anything else. All you need to say is a simple 'Yes' or 'No.' Otherwise you will be condemned." (James 5:12)

The commands "do not swear" have nothing to do with expletives or profanity as it is commonly believed, but they have everything to do with the fact that when we speak something as a vow or oath, we are doing so *in God's name*. The Lord takes these invocations seriously. Note the words of Jesus from His Sermon on the Mount in the context of Satan our enemy and accuser: anything other than "Yes" or "No" comes *from the evil one*, while James adds that wrongly-made vows will *condemn* us.

Like everything in our world after the Fall, we now have

good and bad realities in all areas. There are good oaths and bad oaths just like there is good shame and bad shame. Oaths can be constructive or destructive.

> There are good oaths and bad oaths just like there is good shame and bad shame.

When I was a teacher at Tucson's Catalina High School in the mid-1970s, I was offered a contract at the end of a school year that gave educators a raise for the following year of just over one percent. When I received my contract, I was happy with that raise and I signed and returned it to the district office. When I came back to school to start classes for the fall semester, officials with the teacher's union were up in arms. They felt the district did not negotiate the raise in good faith—and began preparations to have the teachers go out on strike. A friend who worked at the city's fire department and was familiar with unions and strikes advised me to make my mind up right away about whether or not I was going to join the picket lines. "If you are at all wishy-washy about whether or not to go on strike," he added, "the union will bring all pressure to bear."

I signed my contract. Therefore, I made an oath that I was going to fulfill my teaching duties in the coming year at the pay rate offered. It was a promise based on my word. As far as I was concerned, it was as though I did it in God's name. I was approached by a union representative and asked if I was going to go on strike. I told him "No."

"Don't you understand," he said, "that the district didn't negotiate fairly?"

"Perhaps," I responded. "But I signed my contract. It is done. I am not going to break my word."

He cocked an eyebrow. "What if fifty-one percent of the teachers vote to go out on strike?"

I stiffened my back. "Fifty-one percent don't tell me what's right or wrong. I will not violate my word." With that, he walked away—and I was never approached again. The teachers did go out on strike for one month, and in that time other colleagues who did not strike were criticized or threatened, but it never happened to me.

God wants us to be people of our word as regents of the Lord and as His image bearers. This is what Jesus meant when He said, "Whatever you bind on earth will be bound in heaven, and whatever you loose on earth will be loosed in heaven." (Matthew 18:18) That's why it's vital, then, that when we do make an oath, *we only do so about things we can control.* This goes back to goals and desires. If we want something that we can control, it's a goal; if we want something that we cannot control, it's a desire. Examples of good oaths we can control are the ones we make in a court of law ("I swear to tell the truth, the whole truth, and nothing but the truth, so help me, God.") or traditional marriage vows. A bad oath we cannot control, for instance, is to say after a relationship break-up, "I swear I will never love someone ever again." Therefore, in the area of repentance, if we say to God or to someone that we will "never" sin again, that's not a goal that we can control. It's a desire that we cannot control; after all, we're not perfect.

However, if we say that we will do everything in our power to not sin again, that's a goal we can control because our ability to fulfill that commitment is based on our behavior.

Satan's role in our oaths is illustrated well in Mark 6 with the story of Herod the tetrarch. He had John the Baptist arrested because of John's public condemnation of Herod's brother Philip and Philip's unlawful relationship with his wife Herodias. We're even told that Herod wanted to kill John, but was afraid to do so because the people considered John to be a prophet. This led Herod, spurred by unnatural lust, to make an oath that entrapped him:

> "Finally the opportune time came. On his birthday Herod gave a banquet for his high officials and military commanders and the leading men of Galilee. When the daughter of Herodias came in and danced, she pleased Herod and his dinner guests. The king said to the girl, 'Ask me for anything you want, and I'll give it to you.' And he promised her with an oath, 'Whatever you ask I will give you, up to half my kingdom.' She went out and said to her mother, 'What shall I ask for?' 'The head of John the Baptist,' she answered. At once the girl hurried in to the king with the request: 'I want you to give me right now the head of John the Baptist on a platter.' The king was greatly distressed, but because of his oaths and his dinner guests, he did not want to refuse her. So he immediately sent an executioner with orders to bring John's head. The man went, beheaded John in the prison, and brought back

his head on a platter. He presented it to the girl, and she gave it to her mother." (Mark 6:21-28)

Satan used Herod's lust to cause him to make an oath that bound him to evil—and the same thing can happen to us if we make oaths about matters or desires we cannot control. Thankfully, we have a way to break this bondage and be free from its evil impact. It's revealed in the Old Testament.

"Moses said to the heads of the tribes of Israel: 'This is what the Lord commands: When a man makes a vow to the Lord or takes an oath to obligate himself by a pledge, he must not break his word but must do everything he said. When a young woman still living in her father's household makes a vow to the Lord or obligates herself by a pledge and her father hears about her vow or pledge but says nothing to her, then all her vows and every pledge by which she obligated herself will stand. But if her father forbids her when he hears about it, none of her vows or the pledges by which she obligated herself will stand; the Lord will release her because her father has forbidden her. If she marries after she makes a vow or after her lips utter a rash promise by which she obligates herself and her husband hears about it but says nothing to her, then her vows or the pledges by which she obligated herself will stand. But if her husband forbids her when he hears about it, he nullifies the vow that obligates her or the rash promise by which she obligates herself, and the Lord will release her.'" (Numbers 30:1-8)

Do you see the crossover? In Old Testament times, the father or the husband could override a vow. In the same way, our Heavenly Father (because we are children of God) and our spiritual husband Jesus (because we are a part of the church, the bride of Christ) can nullify the oaths we cannot control when we bring them to Him in confession and repentance.

God wants us to be people of our word as regents of the Lord and as His image bearers.

Confession and repentance are the keys to living in the freedom God has afforded to us as His image bearers. The pathway to renouncing a vow we should never have made, or of not making a foolish vow to begin with, is found in Leviticus 5:5 – **"so it shall be when he becomes guilty in one of these, that he shall confess that in which he has sinned"**. We are to confess we have sinned in making such a statement and vow. Admit our sin. The second part goes to what James says in James 4:7. It says, **"Submit yourselves, then, to God. Resist the devil, and he will flee from you."** Jesus, of course, modeled this pathway for us in the Garden of Gethsemane in Luke 22:42: "Father, if you are willing, take this cup from me; yet not my will, but yours be done." He submitted by confessing His fear and desire to the Lord ("take this cup from me..."), and resisted the devil and made him flee by confirming His submission ("...yet not my will, but yours be done."). Jesus did not make any oath at all in the garden; He simply submitted.

I had to do this in a most poignant way when my son John

was in the United States Army in Germany getting ready to depart for Iraq. It was in early 2006 and Susie and I flew there to see him and his wife prior to his deployment to the Middle East. Before we left, Susie wisely said that when we got there, we needed to address our fears and give them over to the Lord. As the four of us met, we asked John, "What is your greatest fear." He said that it was not death. John has a warrior mentality; he always told me, "Dad, the bullet that is going to kill me is already known by God, so until then, I have nothing to fear." So he wasn't afraid to die. His fear, though, was that he'd survive but return home a quadriplegic and paralyzed. The rest of us agreed with his fear, but added that we were also afraid that he could perish in battle. It was a sobering time.

Our fears expressed, we then prayed together. "Lord," I said, "we do not want John to die, become a quadriplegic, or be paralyzed. But you are God. We submit to your will for our son. Even if you want to go there with him, we will go there with you. It will be painful and difficult, but we are willing to go there with you because you will walk with us through it." We made no oaths, and we didn't try to make a deal with God. We simply submitted. To this day, it was the hardest prayer I've ever spoken.

Once we returned home, John was sent to Iraq and led a Brigade Reconnaissance Platoon of the U.S. Army First Armored Division into the second Battle of Ramadi from April to November 2006. Many days came when I wondered if John was okay and I'd have to remember our shared submission to God and reaffirm it. Each time I did, I resisted the devil and he fled. He didn't stay away, of course. Like he did with Cain, he often crouched at my door and tempted me to sin. Satan always returns to try to undermine our faith and even get us to make an oath we cannot keep. But every time he showed up, I affirmed our submission, he was resisted, and then he departed. In the end, God protected John through some very dangerous situations and he was not killed or wounded. In fact, he earned two Bronze Stars, but he hardly recognizes the honor because five men in his platoon paid the ultimate sacrifice.

> We made no oaths, and we didn't try to
> make a deal with God. We simply submitted.

Conversely, in Judges 11 we are introduced to Jephthah the Gileadite, identified as "a mighty warrior" who also led his men into the perils of battle, but instead of submitting his fears to God, he made a deal with the Lord—and a bad oath in the process.

"And Jephthah made a vow to the Lord: 'If you give the Ammonites into my hands, whatever comes out of the door of my house to meet me when I return in triumph from the Ammonites will be the Lord's, and I will sacrifice it as a burnt offering.' Then Jephthah went over to fight the Ammonites, and the Lord gave them into his hands. He devastated twenty towns from Aroer to the vicinity of Minnith, as far as Abel Keramim. Thus Israel subdued Ammon. When Jephthah returned to his home in Mizpah, who should come out to meet him but his daughter, dancing to the sound of timbrels! She was an only child. Except for her he had neither son nor daughter. When he saw her, he tore his clothes and cried, 'Oh no, my daughter! You have brought me down and I am devastated. I have made a vow to the Lord that I cannot break.' 'My father,' she replied, 'you have given your word to the Lord. Do to me just as you promised, now that the Lord has avenged you of your enemies, the Ammonites. But grant me this one request,' she said. 'Give me two months to roam the hills and weep with my friends, because I will never marry.' 'You may go,' he said. And he let her go for two months. She and her friends went into the hills and wept because she would never marry. After the two months, she returned to her father, and he did to her as he had vowed." (Judges 11:31-40a)

What a sad epitaph to a story that didn't have to turn out the way it did. When Jephthah declared to his daughter, "I have made a vow to the Lord that I cannot break," that's not true. Remember Numbers 30? At the very moment his girl walked out of the tent, Jephthah could've confessed and renounced the oath. "Lord, I made a foolish vow to you," he could've prayed. "I ask you to forbid my oath, nullify my rash promise, and I will submit to whatever you desire me to do." But he didn't. In fact, when he told his daughter, "You have brought me down," he deflected the blame and responsibility for his own actions onto *her*. Incredibly, she still wanted her father to honor his vow. She's her daddy's girl and respected him to the very end of her life. Jephthah's tale vividly displays why Jesus said in the Sermon on the Mount, "All you need to say is simply 'Yes' or 'No'; anything beyond this comes from the evil one." Satan will use the oaths we shouldn't have made to ruin us, ruin those around us impacted by the vow, and bring destruction and even death.

> Confession and repentance are the keys
> to living in the freedom God has afforded
> to us as His image bearers.

We must be careful when we are hurting or scared or shamed of the oaths we make and be willing to renounce them through confession and repentance. After all, confession and repentance are the keys to living in the freedom God has afforded to us as His image bearers. But as we interact with others to help them recognize *their* need for confession and repentance, we often make a tragic mistake; one we must correct—for lives are being lost for eternity in the meantime.

Chapter 9

FREEDOM

One afternoon in Kenya, I was riding on the matatu with my boss from The Navigators, Mutua Mahiaini. We sat down next to a young man who, after exchanging pleasantries with Mutua, launched into a presentation of the Gospel. He laid out the Romans Road (Romans 3:23, Romans 6:23, Romans 5:8, Romans 10:9,10) path to salvation in Jesus stone by stone in a well-presented but also well-rehearsed discourse that went on for thirty laborious minutes.

When he finally closed with a confident request of Mutua to pray to receive Christ as Savior and Lord, Mutua smiled politely and revealed that he was already a believer in Jesus. Sadly, the young man never once stopped to ask Mutua what he thought, what he was going through in life at that moment, or even if he believed in God to begin with. Instead, he spent a half hour delivering an impersonal, non-conversational monologue to the national leader of a worldwide Christian ministry.

Many of us who consider ourselves to be evangelical Christians have an unfortunate tendency in our interactions with other people. Our presentation of the Gospel is primarily, if not exclusively, focused on the confession and forgiveness of their sins. We ignore the fact that not everyone is struggling with the guilt of their own sin; rather, many are struggling with the pain caused by sins done *against* them. This tendency narrows the fullness of the Gospel and results in many people not being dealt with individually and personally at a heart level—and therefore not coming to faith in God.

The Gospel, by definition, is the teaching or revelation of Christ and is referred to in the Bible as the "good news." Used often in Matthew, Mark, Luke, and Acts, this term is perhaps most familiar in this passage from Isaiah 61.

"The Spirit of the Sovereign Lord is on me, because the Lord has anointed me to proclaim good news to the poor. He has sent me to bind up the brokenhearted, to proclaim freedom for the captives and release from darkness for the prisoners, to proclaim the year of the Lord's favor." (Isaiah 61:1-2a)

Considered to be a prophetic announcement of how the Son of God would inaugurate the kingdom of God on Earth, notice how the passage begins with a proclamation of the good news "to the poor." That matches nicely with Jesus' very first words from the Beatitudes in Matthew 5: "Blessed are the poor in spirit, for theirs is the kingdom of heaven." Then Isaiah's words follow with the exhortation "to bind up the brokenhearted," a direct companion to Jesus' next words in His sermon, "Blessed are those who mourn, for they will be comforted." Finally, the pronouncement in this passage to bring "freedom for the captives and release from darkness for the prisoners" ties perfectly well with others Jesus addressed in Matthew 5 who may be in bondage to any manner of things from their words (oaths) to an addiction.

Jesus' sacrifice also fully covers the pain and wounds caused in our lives by the sins of others against us.

Do you see the emphasis? There is no doubt Christ's death of the cross paid the price for the sins of humanity. It covered the guilt of our sins in His blood. But Jesus' sacrifice also fully covers the pain and wounds caused in our lives by the sins of others against us. God wants to comfort, heal, and restore us from *all* of the ravages of sin. No wonder, then, Isaiah earlier wrote in another prophetic foreshadowing of Christ, "But he was pierced for our transgressions, he was crushed for our iniquities; the punishment that brought us peace was on him, and by his wounds we are healed." (Isaiah 53:5) The conclusion of the passage is not limited to physical healing. It addresses the totality of the wounds we experience in this life. Jesus' sacrifice covers them all!

Henry Blackaby's *Experiencing God* speaks of how the Lord invites us to become involved with Him in His work, much as Christ did in doing the Father's work during His earthly ministry. I like that emphasis. It exhorts us to discern where God is *at work* in other people's lives and then address that need in our ministry to them. We must set aside the predisposition to first "get them saved" via the confession and forgiveness of their sins. Instead, our focus should be to discern exactly what God is doing in their lives. Is He working to help them learn to trust Jesus with their pain from the sins committed against them? Oftentimes, His healing for their pain will draw them to the Lord as much as, if not more so, than the focus on the guilt about their own sins.

Don't misunderstand. I'm not trumpeting a call to tepid "friendship evangelism" where we get to know someone else so well that we never challenge them to consider a relationship with God. I am, however, saying that we need to understand that the application of the "good news" encompasses a far wider perspective on the human condition than we have been led to believe by our theology and our practice of Christianity. We have a Romans Road for the person who feels the guilt of their sin, but we lack a Romans Road for the person struggling with the horrors of any hideous sin committed against them. What does the Bible have to say to them?

Let's return again to Paul's words to the Corinthians.

"Praise be to the God and Father of our Lord Jesus Christ, the Father of compassion and the God of all comfort, who comforts us in all our troubles, so that we can comfort those in any trouble with the comfort we ourselves receive from God." (2 Corinthians 1:3-4)

Do you see the emphasis? God comforts us so that we can comfort those in trouble. Yet we can tend to only offer others

His message of forgiveness for their sins and not offer His message of healing for the *effect* of other's sins upon them. Is it possible that we do this because we have not allowed the Lord to comfort our own wounds? Paul adds in verse 6 of that passage that "if we are distressed, it is for your comfort and salvation." In other words, Paul had allowed God to work through his pain and hurts so that he could offer both comfort and salvation to others. Have we allowed the Lord to do this in us?

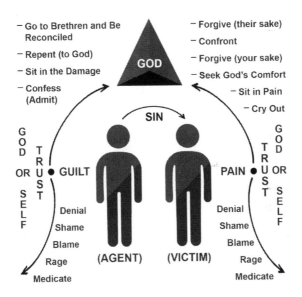

My wife teaches Survey of the Old Testament to freshman students at Desert Christian. Every year she asks them a compelling question, "What are Christians known for?" Every year, she gets the same response from many of the kids, most of whom have been brought up in Christian homes and have attended church for as long as they can remember: "Christians should be known for being right." It's a fascinating observation of what we as parents (and the evangelical church as a whole) have communicated to our young people. We should be known for our *correctness*, they say, and for our ability to tell right from wrong and do what is *right*. It's a fairly legalistic mindset that stems, at least in part, from the theological arguments that remain prevalent among many believers in Christ. Yet I always tell my students that there won't be a theology quiz to get into Heaven. We have the promise of eternal life in Heaven on the basis of the work of Christ in our lives and our decision to trust in Him, not on getting everything right. So what *should* Christians be known for? For being people who rely upon and trust in God, made manifest in the love we display to others as we offer both comfort and salvation. As Paul declared in Galatians 5:6, "For in Christ Jesus neither circumcision nor uncircumcision has any value. The only thing that counts is faith expressing itself through love."

> God comforts us so that we can
> comfort those in trouble.

As believers in God, I believe we need a worldview change to understand that the whole "good news" speaks to both of these issues; a holistic gospel that meets the needs of both the body and the spirit, where we see others and ask ourselves, "Where is God at work in them, and how can I bring trusting in Him to help them address that area?" There is an error in our thinking in that we compartmentalize the sacred from the secular. I'll ask high school students, "What is more spiritual? Doing a Bible study or doing your algebra homework?" Of course, they say its Bible study—but that's simply not true. Any task we do as believers in Christ is equally spiritual and equally sacred in the eyes of God. We need to realize that God is active in everything that we do, and He is to be manifested to others through all that we do.

This is the way Jesus Christ lived. All was sacred, and He dealt with everyone He encountered in the totality of their humanness. If they had a physical need, He brought healing to that need and then said, "Trust in me," not the other way around. I'm optimistic that there is a growing awareness to reject the sacred-secular split in our mentality and in our practice of Christianity. We've communicated to people that it's when we get to Heaven that God will wipe away all of our tears. That's absolutely true. But does that mean that between now and then that there's nothing God wants to do to bring healing to wipe away the tears we're experiencing today or tomorrow or next week? That's not the "good news" at all! God wants to save you now *and* He wants to comfort you now.

Back when I was in Kenya, I learned how to play squash. Essentially, it's like tennis played on a racquetball court, and after my return to the States I started a weekly game with a friend who is a land developer and an immigrant from Latin America. As we developed our friendship while playing the sport, I strived to keep in mind the idea that my interaction with him was a sacred task and not separated from the spiritual in any way. We'd competed against one another pretty much every week over a six-year period before one day during a break between sets he asked me, "John, are you one of them born again Christians?"

I smiled as I toweled my brow. "Yeah, you can categorize me as someone like that. Why do you ask?"

"If you're one of those," he replied, "then why haven't you tried to convert me?"

He then went one to share how he took his mother with terminal cancer, at her request, to a healing crusade in Anaheim, California held by Benny Hinn. He said it was his first exposure to born again Christians, and he noted how the services were focused not so much on healing but on getting attendees to accept Jesus as Lord. He and his mother stayed for two days before coming home. She died six weeks later. Yet he wasn't bitter that she hadn't been healed. He was more puzzled as to why I hadn't tried to get him saved.

"Well," I said, "first of all, I don't convert anybody. That's a situation between you and God, not something I do to you." For the next half-hour, we talked about God and faith, and in the course of the conversation, I asked him, "Have you ever felt like God is trying to get your attention?" He immediately nodded and then told me about his younger brother who had a drug addiction and the pain that he felt from the feeling that he couldn't protect his brother from its destruction. Interestingly, it was through a hurtful situation that he believed God was trying to get his attention. Ask others the same question and you will find that they'll often bring up a painful circumstance as well. That's when you can encourage them to trust God with that pain. I no longer play squash with my friend, but I still stay in touch with him—and I'm not worried about him at all. I know that God is at work in His life.

The late Dallas Willard was a professor in the School of Philosophy at the University of Southern California in Los Angeles from 1965 until shortly before his death in 2013. His lectures and books on Christianity were significant. One of the subjects he talked about was the "vampire Christian," the idea that if we just get a little bit of the blood of Jesus on us, we can proceed to live our lives the way that we want. He emphasized, though, that to consciously acknowledge salvation, but not allow it to have anything to do with the reality of how we live is not only unbiblical but almost an agnostic concept. We have to move beyond simple mental ascent of the idea of salvation to an act of the will in our hearts to actually *live* what we believe. Yet so often we declare to others, "Just repeat the sinner's prayer and you can rest assured you're not going to Hell. You're *in*. That's all you need to do." The result of this incomplete application of our witness for Jesus is the creation of those Willard labeled as 'vampire Christians'.

God is active in everything that we do,
and He is to be manifested to others
through all that we do.

In John 14:15, Jesus' words are clear: "If you love me, keep my commands." As Christians, we must address the will of the other person, not merely their mental ascent. Their salvation in God and love for Him is shown by their willfulness to choose to obey and do what God says, and to trust and rely on the Lord. We must help them to see that they need to decide to bow their will to the will of God and to trust Him with their pain or guilt. Just saying a prayer or agreeing to a doctrinal position is not enough. Willard refers to the required progression as vision to intention to means. Vision is the mental ascent to believe God, intention is the decision to obey God, and means is the way by which obedience is carried out.

As a freshman in college, I was roommates with my cousin. He flunked out in his freshman year and ended up being drafted into the U.S. Army and sent to sunny South Vietnam in 1970. We stayed in contact by mail, and after he had been there for four months, I received a return letter from him in which he described a firefight his unit had with the Viet Cong. He told me a mortar shell had landed about ten feet away from him and blown up. The kill zone of the blast and shrapnel from those shells was twenty yards, but he said he'd been blown through the air for thirty feet—and was uninjured, other than two ruptured eardrums. There wasn't a mark on him. Unable to explain what had happened, he wrote, "For the first time in my life, I wonder if there's a God?"

I wrote him back. "Yes, this is God knocking at your door. God is trying to get your attention. He's very gracious to let you know that He is in control of your circumstances, and He has allowed this that you might turn to Him."

He never wrote back. I saw him later after he returned from Vietnam. By then, he was addicted to drugs. I asked him about our correspondence and his wondering about the existence of God. "Yeah," he said, "I thought that for awhile, but I decided that God's not real." It was an act of his will to say, "In light of what I see, I'm choosing not to believe this." Mentally, he could ascent to the miraculous, but he could not bend his will to choose to seek after God. As disheartening as that was, there is hope—because God is greater than us and continues to pursue each of us. Our stories are not yet over.

We have to move beyond simple mental ascent of the idea of salvation to an act of the will in our hearts to actually *live* what we believe.

It is this journey that is at the very core of all of us. God is at work to draw us to Himself so we learn to trust Him with our guilt and pain, grow in love with Him, and obey Him. That is not just mental assent. As James 2:17 reminds us, "faith by itself, if it is not accompanied by action, is dead." As believers in Jesus Christ, let's do all we can to ensure those to whom we witness are not just given the sinner's prayer to address the guilt of their sins; instead, let's also discern where they are with God and where He is working and offer truth spoken in love to their heart of need. Be it a call to repentance of sin to the comfort of God's healing for the pain of the sins committed against them. Indeed, their journey is not yet over.

Chapter 10

Transformation in Community

There is one last danger in our modern era that concerns me as you've read this book. I fear that you will feel that all you need to do is to get by yourself, go before God completely on your own, and have Him comfort you in your pain or deal with you in your guilt so that you can go from there. We have so many self-help books today—*Fourteen Hops to Happiness,* where if you just do these things, your life will turn around and everything will be fine—because we live in a self-centered, narcissistic culture where the focus is on what you can do for yourself to make yourself happy, whole, and healed.

I don't want this book to simply be an addition to your self-help library. Truth is you can't do it alone, nor should you.

I'm a firm believer that dealing with guilt and pain is best approached within a community. Hebrews 10:24,25 calls us to **"Let us consider how to stir up one another to love and good deeds."** A prime example is seen in how the people of

Emanuel African Methodist Episcopal Church in downtown Charleston, South Carolina dealt with the mass shooting that took nine lives on the evening of June 17, 2015. A young troubled man came into the church during a prayer meeting of 12 saints from the church. After an hour sitting there this young man got up and started shooting and killed 9 people. That was a horrific, painful, and evil action that took place in that community when you think that the young man Dylann Roof could sit there, see the love within that community, and then still choose to stand up, take his gun, and kill people. The pain that community suffered is real and definite. But it was so fascinating how they handled it. The evidence of their willingness to sit in their pain and, in the midst of that, offer forgiveness and approach the healing as a community was utterly remarkable. The members of the church did not go off by themselves to deal with the pain; they came together within a community setting.

> God knows you need community
> to address guilt and pain.

God does not want you to have to deal with the pain and the guilt you face in your life all alone.

It's unfortunate that many Protestants tend to look down on the Catholic sacrament of confession. Many Protestants have told me, "We don't need a priest to forgive us; we have Jesus." That is correct but also incomplete. James 5:16 begins with the words, "Therefore confess your sins to each other…" There is an important aspect of you being able to confess your sins within a community. Then James 5:16 continues, "...and pray for each other so that you may be healed." There is something therapeutic and miraculous in confessing our sins to each other *and* praying for each other to be healed. Our individualistic and autonomous culture looks at the things you can do all by yourself. But when you look at all of the twelve-step programs, they begin with broken and hurting people publically admitting their brokenness and their guilt to each other. They've tapped into a truth; God knows you need community to address guilt and pain. James 5:16 dramatically connects both confession and healing together in the context of community.

Earlier I mentioned my friends John and Patti Cepin and their ministry "Potter's Wheel." They bring small groups of people together for a five-day time period of learning, modeling, and practicing the taste of community soul care, of how to bring into the light our sin and pain and allow God's spirit to show grace through the community to address them. These gatherings are similar to the ones that early Methodist groups of the eighteenth century did that created little platoons of believers who held each other accountable to grow and mature as Christians. These groups come together to tell their stories, confess their sins to one another, and pray for one another in a safe and accepting atmosphere. They receive the reflections of other people to the events and circumstances that have marked ones life, and get a chance to interpret and rethink those experiences in a community where they are comforted, challenged, and helped in dealing with their pain and guilt. It is powerful!

My passion is to see this type of dynamic become common-place in every church in America. In *The Theology of Dallas Willard: Discovering Protoevangelical Faith*, by Gary Black Jr. , the author says of Willard's view, "Congregations should look and feel much like hospitals, places where people gather to find healing, honest reflection, and feedback, restorative therapeutic assistance, wisdom, correction, and guidance towards regaining the functionality of their intended destiny." That is a mouthful! Making that the practice of our small groups would revolutionize our lives. Most evangelicals will turn to Acts 2:42 as their definition of how the church should operate: "They devoted themselves to the apostles' teaching and to fellowship, to the breaking of bread and to prayer." But this is a historical report on what the early church *did*; it was never intended to be set up as a doctrinal position. Martin Luther, in fact, defined church is to be a place where the Word of God is taught and the sacraments are delivered, citing Acts 2:42 as a text related to it.

I believe Christian churches should not be places filled with spectators who are being taught and then sent home for the week; instead, it should be a place where people are reminded of God in his glory, His good news Gospel of the Kingdom and encouraged to be honestly involved in helping each other, a refuge where Black cites Willard as saying, "followers of Christ hold one another lovingly accountable in discerning the level and the presence of intentionality to follow Christ." This rarely happens within the modern-day church community, yet "without relationship and community," Black states from Willard, "one can escape the vital reality of submitting their will."

Confession to another person is actually a spiritual discipline. Community is also a spiritual discipline. It is something to be learned that offers "the opportunity for introspection and contemplation for the purposes of evaluation. Individually, and in relationship to others in the body of Christ, disciples first begin the process of uncovering the nature of who they are, good and bad, their feelings, thoughts, habits, and will, social relations and bodily dispositions, that often stand against their intention to obey Christ," says Black of Willard.

Confession and doing these things in community is vital for the development of your Christian character so that you are *consistently undermined* in your tendency to be willfully disobedient. In one Potter's Wheel, there was a person who was sexually abused as a child by a parent. This person had carried the pain and the scarring of that series of events throughout their life. In the midst of that person sharing their story, one of the other people in the group asked, "Have you ever forgiven the parent for what they did to you?" The initial response was "yes," but after additional questioning the person admitted they had never gone before God to seek forgiveness for the parent. Why? The person believed that if God forgave the parent, there was never going to be a price to be paid for what the parent did. The person's theology was all wrong. In response, the group then affirmed the biblical truth that each person does face God and is held accountable for their sins; they don't get off scot free. It took the *community* for this to be understood so that the person could then forgive the parent before God. You see, *authentic community was required* to address the willful disobedience not to forgive.

When we're dealing with sin alone, it's easy to accept our own motives for disobedience to be allowable or even good and justified, despite the scriptural truth that "a person's ways seem pure to them, but motives are weighed by the Lord." (Proverbs 16:2)

In our churches, then, I exhort you to be proactive in seeking out others within your church body and then *with them* creating a community where stories are told, people are lovingly and honestly treated, and healing can occur on a deep and personal level. Typically, small groups in churches start with chit-chat and maybe an opening prayer, followed by an individual leading a topical Bible study with some doctrinal discussion, and then perhaps a closing prayer and more social time. Seldom do these groups dig a little deeper to actually *apply* what was taught to anyone's life, and even then, there usually isn't a comfort level or permission given to openly share and then accept the "stirring up of one another to love and good works" in a safe atmosphere. At the very least, the Bible study should be the jumping off point from which the group then asks each other, "What is the Spirit of God stirring in your heart related to this?" or "What is God trying to accomplish in your life—or in mine?"

Church small groups need to become real places where real people share real stories with one another in honest transparency so that questions can be asked, reflections offered, and lives impacted and healed. This is when our churches will become the hospitals Willard spoke of and your faith and trust in God will be challenged and will become relevant to you and to those around you in that group.

In addition to *The Theology of Dallas Willard: Discovering Protoevangelical Faith*, I also recommend as essential resources Larry Crabb's *Encouragement: The Key to Caring* and Dan Allender's *To Be Told* for developing your small group into a soul care community. You'll also find *A Long Obedience in the Same Direction* by Eugene Peterson and *The Land Between: Finding God in Difficult Transitions* by Jeff Manion to be valuable.

Made in the USA
San Bernardino, CA
26 August 2017